LIFE IN THE UK TEST

BUMPER EDITION

COMPLETE AND UPDATED OFFICIAL STUDY MATERIAL

REVISION GUIDE

21 COMPLETE TESTS OFFICIAL STYLE

OVER 500 QUESTIONS

7TH EDITION - 2023

DUX
PUBLISHING

TABLE OF CONTENT

What is this guide about?   5
The values and principles of the UK   6
The Life in the UK test   7
Type of questions   9
How to use this book   10

OFFICIAL COURSE MATERIAL

A long and illustrious history   17
    Early Britain   17
    The Middle Ages   20
    The Tudors and Stuarts   24
    A global power   30
    The 20th century   40
    Britain since 1945   44
A modern, thriving society
    The UK today   53
    Religion   56
    Customs and traditions   57
    Sport   60
    Arts and culture   64
    Leisure   71
    Places of interest   76
The UK government, the law and your role
    The development of British democracy   83
    The British constitution   84
    The government   88
    Who can vote?   92
    The UK and international institutions   96
    Respecting the law   98
    The role of the courts   100
    Fundamental principles   104
    Taxation   106
    Driving   107
    Your role in the community   108
    How you can support your community   109

REVISION NOTES

Monarchs 116

Key Dates 119

Important people 123

TESTS

Test 1 127

Test 2 133

Test 3 139

Test 4 145

Test 5 151

Test 6 157

Test 7 163

Test 8 169

Test 9 175

Test 10 181

Test 11 187

Test 12 193

Test 13 199

Test 14 205

Test 15 211

Test 16 217

Test 17 223

Test 18 229

Test 19 235

Test 20 241

Test 21 247

The detailed answers to each questions can be found at the end of every test.

WHAT IS THIS GUIDE ABOUT?

Are you looking to become a British citizen or to settle in the UK? Then if you are aged between 18 and 65 you will need to pass the Life in the UK test.

The test consists of many questions about the history of the UK, the country's traditions and customs as well as the rules of modern politics and institutions. You probably bought the book to study at your own pace. I have added illustrations and little info bubbles throughout to help you. At the end of each chapter, you will also find a list of the key points to remember and understand. These lists are not exhaustive but they help you remember what the chapter was about.

Finally, you can practice the test at your own rhythm with 21 mock exam that follow the exact format of the official test. Just remember to set a clock or a stopwatch to measure your time and see how you progress as you run through the 504 questions.

Please, do check out the Audio version of this book. Sometimes, it is very useful to hear the text you are reading to remember it better.

Seventh Edition 2023
A few changes were made this year:
- Course material updated
- Course material fully illustrated.
- Tests updated

The values and principles of the UK

British society is founded on fundamental values and principles which all those living in the UK should respect and support. These values are reflected in the responsibilities, rights and privileges of being a British citizen or permanent resident of the UK. They are based on history and traditions and are protected by law, customs and expectations. There is no place in British society for extremism or intolerance.

The fundamental principles of British life include:
- Democracy
- The rule of law
- Individual liberty
- Tolerance of those with different faiths and beliefs
- Participation in community life.

As part of the citizenship ceremony, new citizens pledge to uphold these values.

The pledge is:

'I will give my loyalty to the United Kingdom and respect its rights and freedoms. I will uphold its democratic values. I will observe its laws faithfully and fulfil my duties and obligations as a British citizen.'

The citizenship ceremony also request the new British citizen to take either an Oath of allegiance or an Affirmation of allegiance. By the Oath, you swear by Almighty God whereas with the Affirmation, you solemnly, sincerely and truly declare your allegiance to His Majesty King Charles the Third, his Heirs and Successors, according to law.

Flowing from the fundamental principles are responsibilities and freedoms which are shared by all those living in the UK and which we expect all residents to respect.

In return, the UK offers:

- freedom of belief and religion
- freedom of speech
- freedom from unfair discrimination
- a right to a fair trial
- a right to join in the election of a government.

The Life in the UK test

Are you looking to become a British citizen and to settle in the UK? Then, if you are aged between 18 and 65 you will need to pass the Life in the UK test. No matter how much you already know about the UK, you will need to sit and pass the test as part of your application to live in the UK. To maximise your chances of passing, you may buy the book and study it either alone, online, in classes, or with a personal teacher. Then, when you are ready you can sit the exam and hopefully pass.

**You do not need to pass the test
if you are under 18 or over 64.**

If you have already passed the test once, you do not need to sit again. For instance, if you have already passed the test to become settled in the UK and are now applying for citizenship, you do not need to sit the test again.

These are the three steps to ensure the best chances of success:

STUDY – BOOK – TAKE

First step: Study British customs, traditions and history

There is no secret here, a test is a test! The more you prepare for it, the greater your chances of success. In this guide, I provide some additional revision lists to help you prepare. You can carry it all with you in your kindle, on your phone, everywhere you want but be careful, you will not be allowed to take it to the test centre!

In the next few pages, I will give you some tips on the best way to prepare using this book and other resources. But remember that ultimately, you know better than anyone else how you prefer to learn and memorise things.

Second step: Book the test

You must book the test at the very least three days in advance. I would suggest you book it several weeks in advance. This way, it gives you time to study but also a deadline. If you have a tendency to wait until last minute, you may never book the test at all. If you put a date in your calendar, then you know you need to be ready for that date. You can only book the test online! To book a test you need an email address, a debit or credit card, and a valid ID. If going online or using an email address is an issue, your local library, a university, or even a friend might help you with this part of the process.

Book the test online: https://www.lituktestbooking.co.uk/lituk-web/

There are 30 official centres throughout the UK and you need to choose one close to where you live. You can choose among the five closest to you. Do not select another one as you may not be accepted on the day. The test costs £50 independently of date and location. Be careful though, there is no refund so make sure you are making the correct booking and that you actually turn up on the day!

If you have any disabilities or special requirements, you should mention this at the time of booking the test. For any issue, there is a phone helpline available during the week.

Third step: Take the test

The test takes place in a room where no book or assistance materials are allowed. You will need to rely solely on your knowledge and memory. You cannot bring anyone with you. If you travelled with your children for instance, they will have to wait for you outside. Likewise, watches and electronic devices including phones are not accepted in the test room. There are lockers where you can securely leave these devices. Be careful, you will be searched on arrival, and cheating is a serious offence, which would not only void your test, but could also severely limit your application for settlement or citizenship.

When you arrive at the test centre, make sure you bring the following:
- The ID that you used to book the test online
- A proof of address less than 3 months old that shows your name and postcode

Cancellation

It is possible to cancel the test at least three days prior to the booked date. You can cancel online following the same process as you did to book it.

The test itself

There are 24 randomly selected questions about British traditions, history, and customs. You will have 45 minutes to reply to all of them. To be successful you will need to score 75% or more; meaning you must answer at least 18 of the 24 questions correctly. If you fail, you must wait seven days before you can sit and try again. There is no limitation to the amount of times you can sit the test, but you must pay the £50 fee every time.

24 random questions
45 minutes
75% score (= 18 correct answers)

Type of questions

There are four types of questions. See the example below.

1. One choice
The question lists four possible options, only one is correct.

On which day is Saint George celebrated?

    A. 22nd November
    B. 21st April
    C. 23rd April
    D. 1st March

    Answer: C

2. Multiple choice
The question lists four options, and at least two can be correct.

Which TWO of the following group are British Athletes?
    A. Winston Churchill
    B. Mo Farrah
    C. Richard Branson
    D. Dame Kelly Holmes

    Answer: B and D

3. True or false
The question is a statement that is either true or false.

Is the following statement true or false?

The Prime Minister is appointed by the Parliament every 5 years.
    A. TRUE
    B. FALSE

    Answer: B

4. Find the correct statement
The question lists two statements, but only one is correct.

Which of the following statement is correct?

    A. The Wars of the Roses confirmed the independence of Scotland
    B. The Wars of the Roses established Henry Tudor on the throne of England

    Answer: B

How to use this book

A few tips on learning the material, and passing the test.

The Life in the UK Test is no different from many other tests. As you enter the room and sit at the computer to answer the 24 questions, what you need can be summarised in two words: memory and confidence.

Memory is essential for success. The test is first and foremost a test of memory; it will ask you to find answers to questions based on the knowledge you have retained. For instance, if you are asked about the battle of Bosworth, you will need to remember it was fought in 1485. It saw the end of the Wars of Roses, the death of Richard III and the start of the Tudor dynasty by the accession to the throne of Henry VII. All this requires memory.

Confidence is also crucial in making you successful. The last thing you want during the test is to panic and forget names or get confused in the dates.

I will now give you a few tips for both. Before I start, let me remind you of a single truth: hard work pays off. To pass an exam requires you to work at it. Learn, practice, spend some time revising what you know, and you will give yourself the best chances to pass.

Plan your learning
It is a simple trick that works well for many people: create a plan of action before you start learning. Get a deadline, cut the book in chunks of work, establish a routine, include intermediary milestones, test yourself at various points, check that you are on track, etc.

Regular bite size
Learn a little and often. Only a few people manage to learn a lot very fast. That is quite impressive, but not common. For most of us, what works is to progress little by little over some time. Don't put yourself in a position where you must learn the whole book in 2 days! Plan to do a couple of pages every day for a while.

Create a deadline
It may work better if you know there is an end date. For some people, it may be hard to commit to regular work until there is an end date. Then they realise they have to complete by that date. If that is you, what you can do is book the test. Book it weeks in advance, and then plan your learning. You always have the option to cancel if you need it.

Reward yourself
Don't forget to give yourself a little reward every now and then, especially when you achieve some milestone. For instance, if you pass a mock test, or when you finish one chapter of the book.

Divide & conquer
There are a lot of facts in this book. A lot of dates, names, numbers and other snippets of information to retain. Cut them into sections, parts. Don't attempt to learn all at once. For instance, in the history section, don't just learn every date in chronological order. That's way too much. Instead, just focus on a particular period. Like the Wars of the Roses or the Victorian era. Move onto the next section only when you know this one very well.

Pictures

We have all heard it before, a picture is worth a thousand words. Maybe you can draw your own. The book doesn't include that many pictures or photos, but it doesn't stop you from finding others for instance on the Internet. You can also draw your own diagrams to help memorise certain elements.

Practice with a friend or partner

Give the book to someone and let them ask you questions from the text. This can be a fun way to check what you know. Play it like a Trivial Pursuit if you wish.

Speak aloud

We humans tend to remember what we hear more efficiently than what we read. It also works when we are talking to ourselves. Strange as it sounds, let's make use of this faculty.

Record yourself

You can record yourself and then, for instance, listen back during your commute. There are many free apps on smartphones that can help you there.

Right before you go to bed

We tend to retain easily the information we absorb just before we go to sleep. It is quite common to read or listen to something important in bed, then sleep on it.

Start with the end or repeat randomly

An alternative method of learning a long text is to repeat it in reverse! Once you know a section of the book, revise or check your knowledge not in order, but from the end of the chapter, or even randomly.

Understand the meaning

There is no secret here, it is helpful to understand well what you are trying to commit to memory! For instance, the judicial system in the UK can be a bit difficult to grasp, especially if you come from a country that has a different approach. Use a dictionary and websites to read about it more and make sure you really understand how the various courts work.

Listen as you drive, commute, walk in the park...

Driving or taking the train to work can take a fair chunk of our free time. why not use that time in a useful manner? Listen to the audiobook (or your own recording) as you commute. It can sometimes help to walk while listening to the course. A bit like mindfulness, where you focus on the present, on your surroundings, on your sensations. Walking is an activity that often allows us to clear our mind. Then, put on your earplugs and listen to the course. It may help sink it in.

Write it down

It is a simple tip, but sometimes writing the text down helps to commit it to memory. Now, a word of caution: don't attempt to rewrite the whole book, that would take some time! Instead, write down a few notes, essential words, dates, characters etc. A useful tool to learn is a flashcard. For instance, write a word on one side and its definition or what it relates to on the other side. Then read one side and ask yourself the other.

Confidence

Confidence is vital to increase your chance of passing an exam. But it is also quite hard to get if you have test-phobia.

The first thing to note is that if you know the content well, you increase your confidence. It is quite simple: go to a test centre with limited knowledge, and you are likely to panic. Work at it and know it well and you are more likely to feel good.

The test itself will see you sat alone at a computer under supervision. If you are not used to it, familiarise yourself by taking online tests (there are loads!) and getting used to reading on a screen and using the mouse.

Read the question calmly. Make sure you understand what is asked. Especially if it is a true or false statement, make sure it is not, for instance, a double negative (such as: "it is not uncommon" means it is common). Now read the possible answers. Read the question again. If one answer jumps at you, great. If not, try to eliminate any answer you know is incorrect.

If you are still uncertain, trust your instinct. Sometimes we ignore our hunches, but they are often correct.

You can jump to another question and mark this one for later. At the end of the test, you have the possibility to review all the questions and your answers. Now, my advice is to be cautious here... very often, when we doubt a response, we end up changing it wrongly.

Time management

You have 45 minutes for 24 questions. I would suggest you work on 40 minutes. That gives you 5 minutes buffer if you need to review a question or think about one of your answers. It means you have about 1.5 minutes per question. It feels little time, but if you pace yourself, it is actually a lot of time.

It will take you about 3 to 10 seconds to read the question and up to 20 seconds to read the answers. You now have over a minute to pick the answer. It is enough time. Think about it, it will have taken you between 15 and 30 seconds to read this paragraph. If you spend too long on a question, you will panic over the answer. After 1 minute, just move on and come back later.

You

The test is yours. Only you will be facing the computer. Nobody is judging you. Breath, try to relax. Remember, it is just a test, not like you are undergoing heart surgery.

You can sit the test several times. You will pass it.

On the day

Here are a few tips for the day of the test:

- Get to the centre early. They will not admit you last minute, and you should spend a couple of minutes sitting in there, breathing and calming your whole body down.
- Don't take anything you don't need. You will have to leave your wallet, phone etc. in a locker, so go to the centre as light as you can.
- On a hot day, sit for a bit, cool down before entering the room.
- Drink a bit of water before the test.
- Go to the toilets.
- Maybe book in the morning if you can so you don't spend the whole day thinking about it.
- Take tissue with you, you don't want to panic over not being able to blow your nose when you need to.
- Organise something to look forward to, right after the test. Drinks, meet a friend, shopping... like a reward.
- Say hello to the people you meet, say a nice word. First, it never hurts to be polite but also, it gets you in a positive frame of mind.
- Don't revise on the day. Some people like doing it, but if you know your stuff, you know it. Clear your mind for the day.
- Have a nice breakfast or lunch. Give yourself something you like before the test, it will make you feel good.
- If you have to travel to the centre, see if someone can accompany you. Talk with them, but not about the test!

Final words

This book that you have in your hands, on your electronic device or that you are listening to contains 100% of the official course material published by the Home Office and a series of mock exams to help you prepare.

All the books on the Life in the UK test contain the exact same course. The material has been written by the Home Office, and publishers are not authorised to change it. There is no need to buy another Life In the UK book to supplement your learning because you would re-read the same. Instead, browse the web to find useful information. For instance, when locations are quoted, go online to check what they look like. This book will help you, but you are free to get more information from other places too.

There are many websites to help you practice questions. The official writers of the test have to ensure that it is possible to answer their questions with the Life in The UK content only, but it is possible that one rogue question goes through the checks and requires more knowledge. This is rare but is known to have happened. Don't panic, there would only be one like this, and you might know the answer anyway.

This book is available on **Paperback**, **eBook** and **AudioBook**.

The Official Material for the

LIFE IN THE UK TEST

Course developed by the Home Office
and published by the TSO (The Stationery Office).
Updated Jan 2023

Be mindful that legislation and various other aspects may change at any time.
The test itself is based on the course material.

A long and illustrious history

In this chapter you will learn about British history starting from the Stone Age. The beginning focuses on arriving populations which affected the language and religions of Britain. After that the focus is on the development of the Monarchy, church and Parliament. Major battles and significant periods are covered, including the civil war, the industrial revolution and the Empire. There is a lot of information about WWI and WWII and after WWII the chapter focuses on the governments of the UK and devolution in Northern Ireland, Wales and Scotland.

Make sure that you know and understand:
- the early populations of Britain,
- the relationship between the Monarchy and Parliament,
- Protestants and Catholics,
- Britain and the colonies of the Empire,
- how the right to vote developed,
- the Acts of Parliament and other major events,
- all of the dates given in this chapter.

1. Early Britain

The first people to live in Britain were hunter-gatherers, in what we call the Stone Age. For much of the Stone Age, Britain was connected to the continent by a land bridge. People came and went, following the herds of deer and horses which they hunted. Britain only became permanently separated from the continent by the Channel about 10,000 years ago.

The first farmers arrived in Britain about 6,000 years ago. The ancestors of these first farmers probably came from south-east Europe. These people built houses, tombs and monuments on the land. One of these monuments, Stonehenge, still stands in what is now the English county of Wiltshire. Stonehenge was probably a special gathering place for seasonal ceremonies. Other Stone Age sites have also survived. Skara Brae on Orkney, off the north coast of Scotland, is the best preserved prehistoric village in northern Europe, and has helped archaeologists to understand more about how people lived near the end of the Stone Age.

Around 4,000 years ago, people learned to make bronze. We call this period the Bronze Age. People lived in roundhouses and buried their dead in tombs called round barrows. The people of the Bronze Age were accomplished metalworkers who made many beautiful objects in bronze and gold, including tools, ornaments and weapons. The Bronze Age was followed by the Iron Age, when people learned how to make weapons and tools out of iron. People still lived in roundhouses, grouped together into larger settlements, and sometimes defended sites called hill forts. A very impressive hill fort can still be seen today at Maiden Castle, in the English county of Dorset. Most people were farmers, craft workers or warriors. The language they spoke was part of the Celtic language family. Similar languages were spoken across Europe in the Iron Age, and related languages are still spoken today in some parts of Wales, Scotland and Ireland. The people of the Iron Age had a sophisticated culture and economy. They made the first coins to be minted in Britain, some inscribed with the names of Iron Age kings. This marks the beginnings of British history.

The Romans

Julius Caesar led a Roman invasion of Britain in 55 BC. This was unsuccessful and for nearly 100 years Britain remained separate from the Roman Empire. In AD 43 the Emperor Claudius led the Roman army in a new invasion. This time, there was resistance from some of the British tribes but the Romans were successful in occupying almost

Boudica, Queen of the Iceni, fought against the Romans in 60-61 AD

all of Britain. One of the tribal leaders who fought against the Romans was Boudicca, the queen of the Iceni in what is now eastern England. She is still remembered today and there is a statue of her on Westminster Bridge in London, near the Houses of Parliament.

Areas of what is now Scotland were never conquered by the Romans, and the Emperor Hadrian built a wall (see photo) in the north of England to keep out the Picts (ancestors of the Scottish people). Included in the wall were a number of forts. Parts of Hadrian's Wall, including the forts of Housesteads and Vindolanda, can still be seen. It is a popular area for walkers and is a UNESCO (United Nations Education, Scientific and Cultural Organization) World Heritage Site.

Hadrian's Wall - Steven Fruitsmaak, Public domain

The Romans remained in Britain for 400 years. They built roads and public buildings, created a structure of law, and introduced new plants and animals. It was during the 3rd and 4th centuries AD that the first Christian communities began to appear in Britain.

The Anglo-Saxons

The Roman army left Britain in AD 410 to defend other parts of the Roman Empire and never returned. Britain was again invaded by tribes from northern Europe: the Jutes, the Angles and the Saxons. The languages they spoke are the basis of modern-day English. Battles were fought against these invaders but, by about AD 600, Anglo-Saxon kingdoms were established in Britain. These kingdoms were mainly in what is now England. The burial place of one of the kings was at Sutton Hoo in modern Suffolk. This king was buried with treasure and armour, all placed in a ship which was then covered by a mound of earth. Parts of the west of Britain, including much of what is now Wales, and Scotland, remained free of Anglo-Saxon rule.

The Anglo-Saxons were not Christians when they first came to Britain but, during this period, missionaries came to Britain to preach about Christianity. Missionaries from Ireland spread the religion in the north. The most famous of these were St Patrick, who would become the patron saint of Ireland (see patron saints), and St Columba, who founded a monastery on the island of Iona, off the coast of what is now Scotland. St Augustine led missionaries from Rome, who spread Christianity in the south. St Augustine became the first Archbishop of Canterbury (see Religion in Britain today P56).

The Vikings

The Vikings came from Denmark and Norway. They first visited Britain in AD 789 to raid coastal towns and take away goods and slaves. Then, they began to stay and form their own communities in the east of England and Scotland. The Anglo-Saxon kingdoms in England united under King Alfred the Great, who defeated the Vikings. Many of the Viking invaders stayed in Britain – especially in the east and north of England, in an area known as the Danelaw (many places names there, such as Grimsby and Scunthorpe, come from the Viking languages). The Viking settlers mixed with local communities and some converted to Christianity.

Anglo-Saxon kings continued to rule what is now England, except for a short period when there were Danish kings. The first of these was Cnut, also called Canute. In the north, the threat of attack by Vikings had encouraged the people to unite under one king, Kenneth MacAlpin. The term Scotland began to be used to describe that country.

The Norman Conquest

In 1066, an invasion led by William, the Duke of Normandy (in what is now northern France), defeated Harold, the Saxon king of England, at the Battle of Hastings. Harold was killed in the battle. William became king of England and is known as William the Conqueror. The battle is commemorated in a great piece of embroidery, known as the Bayeux Tapestry, which can still be seen in France today.

Bayeux Tapestry - Dan Koehl

The Norman Conquest was the last successful foreign invasion of England and led to many changes in government and social structures in England. Norman French, the language of the new ruling class, influenced the development of the English language as we know it today. Initially the Normans also conquered Wales, but the Welsh gradually won territory back.

The Scots and the Normans fought on the border between England and Scotland; the Normans took over some land on the border but did not invade Scotland. William sent people all over England to draw up lists of all the towns and villages. The people who lived there, who owned the land and what animals they owned were also listed. This was called the Domesday Book. It still exists today and gives a picture of society in England just after the Norman Conquest.

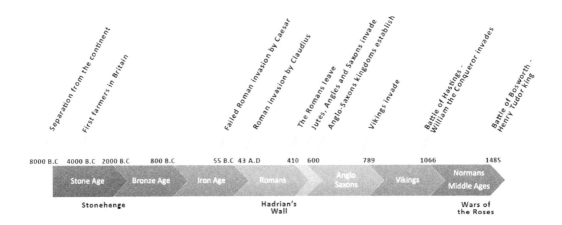

Key points to remember

- The Iron Age marks the start of British History.
- The Romans invade first in 53 BC but fail. They successfully return in 43 AD and remain until 410.
- Successful invasions follow including by the Angles and the Saxons.
- The Vikings come in 709 and mix with local population. They rule England for several centuries.
- The Normans invade in 1066 when William the Conqueror defeats King Harold at Hastings. This is the last successful invasion of the land.

2. The Middle Ages

War at home and abroad

The period after the Norman Conquest up until about 1485 is called the Middle Ages (or the medieval period). It was a time of almost constant war. The English kings fought with the Welsh, Scottish and Irish noblemen for control of their lands. In Wales, the English were able to establish their rule. In 1284 King Edward I of England introduced the Statute of Rhuddlan, which annexed Wales to the Crown of England. Huge castles, including Conwy and Caernarvon, were built to maintain this power. By the middle of the 15th century the last Welsh rebellions had been defeated. English laws and the English language were introduced.

> *Wales is annexed to England in the 13th century and adopts English laws and language by the 15th.*

In Scotland, the English kings were less successful. In 1314 the Scottish, led by Robert the Bruce, defeated the English at the Battle of Bannockburn, and Scotland remained unconquered by the English.

At the beginning of the Middle Ages, Ireland was an independent country. The English first went to Ireland as troops to help the Irish king and remained to build their own settlements. By 1200, the English ruled an area of Ireland known as the Pale, around Dublin. Some of the important lords in other parts of Ireland accepted the authority of the English king.

During the Middle Ages, the English kings also fought a number of wars abroad. Many knights took part in the Crusades, in which European Christians fought for control of the Holy Land. English kings also fought a long war with France, called the Hundred Years War (even though it actually lasted 116 years). One of the most famous battles of the Hundred Years War was the Battle of Agincourt in 1415, where King Henry V's vastly outnumbered English army defeated the French. The English left France in the 1450s.

> *The Hundred Years' War against the French lasted 116 years (1337-1453)*

The Black Death

The Normans used a system of land ownership known as feudalism. The king gave land to his lords in return for help in war. Landowners had to send certain numbers of men to serve in the army. Some peasants had their own land but most were serfs. They had a small area of their lord's land where they could grow food. In return, they had to work for their lord and could not move away. The same system developed in southern Scotland. In the north of Scotland and Ireland, land was owned by members of the 'clans' (prominent families).

In 1348, a disease, probably a form of plague, came to Britain. This was known as the Black Death. One third of the population of England died and a similar proportion in Scotland and Wales. This was one of the worst disasters ever to strike Britain. Following the Black Death, the smaller population meant there was less need to grow cereal crops. There were labour shortages and peasants began to demand higher wages. New social classes appeared, including owners of large areas of land (later called the gentry), and people left the countryside to live in the towns. In the towns, growing wealth led to the development of a strong middle class.

In Ireland, the Black Death killed many in the Pale and, for a time, the area controlled by the English became smaller.

Legal and political changes

In the Middle Ages, Parliament began to develop into the institution it is today. Its origins can be traced to the king's council of advisers, which included important noblemen and the leaders of the Church.

There were few formal limits to the king's power until 1215. In that year, King John was forced by his noblemen to agree to a number of demands. The result was a charter of rights called the Magna Carta (which means the Great Charter). The Magna Carta established the idea that even the king was subject to the law. It protected the rights of the nobility and restricted the king's power to collect taxes or to make or change laws. In future, the king would need to involve his noblemen in decisions.

In England, parliaments were called for the king to consult his nobles, particularly when the king needed to raise money. The numbers attending Parliament increased and two separate parts, known as Houses, were established. The nobility, great landowners and bishops sat in the House of Lords. Knights, who were usually smaller landowners, and wealthy people from towns and cities were elected to sit in the House of Commons. Only a small part of the population was able to join in electing the members of the Commons.

A similar Parliament developed in Scotland. It had three Houses, called Estates: the lords, the commons and the clergy. This was also a time of development in the legal system. The principle that judges are independent of the government began to be established. In England, judges developed 'common law' by a process of precedence (that is, following previous decisions) and tradition. In Scotland, the legal system developed slightly differently and laws were 'codified' (that is, written down).

A distinct identity

The Middle Ages saw the development of a national culture and identity. After the Norman Conquest, the king and his noblemen had spoken Norman French and the peasants had continued to speak Anglo-Saxon. Gradually these two languages combined to become one English language. Some words in modern English – for example, 'park' and 'beauty' – are based on Norman French words. Others – for example, 'apple', 'cow' and 'summer' – are based on Anglo-Saxon words. In modern English there are often words with very similar meanings, one from French and one from Anglo-Saxon. 'Demand' (French) and 'ask' (Anglo-Saxon) are examples. By 1400, in England, official documents were being written in English, and English had become the preferred language of the royal court and Parliament.

English becomes the offical language by 1400.

In the years leading up to 1400, Geoffrey Chaucer wrote a series of poems in English about a group of people going to Canterbury on a pilgrimage. The people decided to tell each other stories on the journey, and the poems describe the travellers and some of the stories they told. This collection of poems is called The Canterbury Tales. It was one of the first books to be printed by William Caxton, the first person in England to print books using a printing press. Many of the stories are still popular. Some have been made into plays and television programmes.

*1400 - Geoffrey Chaucer wrote **The Canterbury Tales** - a series of poems.*

In Scotland, many people continued to speak Gaelic and the Scots language also developed. A number of poets began to write in the Scots language. One example is John Barbour, who wrote The Bruce about the Battle of Bannockburn.

The Middle Ages also saw a change in the type of buildings in Britain. Castles were built in many places in Britain and Ireland, partly for defence. Today many are in ruins, although some, such as Windsor and Edinburgh, are still in use. Great cathedrals – for example, Lincoln Cathedral – were also

York Minster - Matze Trier

built, and many of these are still used for worship. Several of the cathedrals had windows of stained glass, telling stories about the Bible and Christian saints. The glass in York Minster is a famous example.

During this period, England was an important trading nation. English wool became a very important export. People came to England from abroad to trade and also to work. Many had special skills, such as weavers from France, engineers from Germany, glass manufacturers from Italy and canal builders from Holland.

The Wars of the Roses

In 1455, a civil war was begun to decide who should be king of England. It was fought between the supporters of two families: the House of Lancaster and the House of York. This war was called the Wars of the Roses, because the symbol of Lancaster was a red rose and the symbol of York was a white rose. The war ended with the Battle of Bosworth Field in 1485.

King Richard III of the House of York was killed in the battle and Henry Tudor, the leader of the House of Lancaster, became King Henry VII. Henry then married King Richard's niece, Elizabeth of York, and united the two families. Henry was the first king of the House of Tudor. The symbol of the House of Tudor was a red rose with a white rose inside it as a sign that the Houses of York and Lancaster were now allies.

Red Rose of Lancaster   *Tudor Rose*   *White Rose of York*

Tudor rose - By xenial- Adobe Stock (licensed)

Key points to remember

- The Middle Ages start in 5th century, after the Romans leave and lasts until the 15th century, after the Wars of Roses end.
- The Statute of Rhuddlan in 1284 annexes Wales to the Crown of England.
- In 1314,Robert the Bruce defeats the English at the battle of Bannockburn. The victory keeps Scotland independent.
- The English join European forces to fight in Orient during the Crusades.
- The 100 years war with France lasts 116 years (1337–1453). During this time, the English defeat the French at the battle of Agincourt in 1415.
- A form of plague called the Black Death spreads in 1348 and kills a third of the population. A direct consequence is a change in how the land is worked. A new class of citizens appears in people who own the land they work: the Gentry.
- The Magna Carta (1215) reduces the power of the King, making way to the development of Parliament outside of the king's close circle of advisers.

3. The Tudors and Stuarts

Portrait of Henry VIII
After Hans Holbein the Younger

Religious conflicts

After his victory in the Wars of the Roses, Henry VII wanted to make sure that England remained peaceful and that his position as king was secure. He deliberately strengthened the central administration of England and reduced the power of the nobles. He was thrifty and built up the monarchy's financial reserves. When he died, his son Henry VIII continued the policy of centralising power.

Henry VIII was most famous for breaking away from the Church of Rome and marrying six times. To divorce his first wife, Henry needed the approval of the Pope. When the Pope refused, Henry established the Church of England. In this new Church, the king, not the Pope, would have the power to appoint bishops and order how people should worship.

At the same time the Reformation was happening across Europe. This was a movement against the authority of the Pope and the ideas and practices of the Roman Catholic Church. The Protestants formed their own churches. They read the Bible in their own languages instead of in Latin; they did not pray to saints or at shrines; and they believed that a person's own relationship with God was more important than submitting to the authority of the Church. Protestant ideas gradually gained strength in England, Wales and Scotland during the 16th century.

In Ireland, however, attempts by the English to impose Protestantism (alongside efforts to introduce the English system of laws about the inheritance of land) led to rebellion from the Irish chieftains, and much brutal fighting followed.

Henry VIII unites Wales with England.

During the reign of Henry VIII, Wales became formally united with England by the Laws in Wales Acts. The Welsh sent representatives to the House of Commons and the Welsh legal system was reformed.

Henry VIII was succeeded by his son Edward VI, who was strongly Protestant. During his reign, the Book of Common Prayer was written to be used in the Church of England. A version of this book is still used in some churches today. Edward died at the age of 15 after ruling for just over six years, and his half-sister Mary became queen. Mary was a devout Catholic and persecuted Protestants (for this reason, she became known as 'Bloody Mary'). Mary also died after a short reign and the next monarch was her half-sister, Elizabeth, the daughter of Henry VIII and Anne Boleyn.

Queen Elizabeth I

Queen Elizabeth I was a Protestant. She re-established the Church of England as the official Church in England. Everyone had to attend their local church and there were laws about the type of religious services and the prayers which could be said, but Elizabeth did not ask about people's real beliefs. She succeeded in finding a balance between the views of Catholics and the more extreme Protestants. In this way, she avoided any serious religious conflict within England. Elizabeth became one of the most popular monarchs in English history, particularly after 1588, when the English defeated the Spanish Armada (a large fleet of ships), which had been sent by Spain to conquer England and restore Catholicism.

The Ermine Portrait of Elizabeth I of England - Attributed to William Segar

The Reformation in Scotland and Mary, Queen of Scots

Scotland had also been strongly influenced by Protestant ideas. In 1560, the predominantly Protestant Scottish Parliament abolished the authority of the Pope in Scotland and Roman Catholic religious services became illegal.

A Protestant Church of Scotland with a leadership was established but, unlike in England, this was not a state Church.

The queen of Scotland, Mary Stuart (often now called 'Mary, Queen of Scots') was a Catholic. She was only a week old when her father died and she became queen. Much of her childhood was spent in France. When she returned to Scotland, she was the centre of a power struggle between different groups. When her husband was murdered, Mary was suspected of involvement and fled to England. She gave her throne to her Protestant son, James VI of Scotland. Mary was Elizabeth I's cousin and hoped that Elizabeth might help her, but Elizabeth suspected Mary of wanting to take over the English throne, and kept her a prisoner for 20 years. Mary was eventually executed, accused of plotting against Elizabeth I.

Exploration, poetry and drama

The Elizabethan period in England was a time of growing patriotism: a feeling of pride in being English. English explorers sought new trade routes and tried to expand British trade into the Spanish colonies in the Americas. Sir Francis Drake, one of the commanders in the defeat of the Spanish Armada, was one of the founders of England's naval tradition. His ship, the Golden Hind, was one of the first to sail right around ('circumnavigate') the world. In Elizabeth I's time, English settlers first began to colonise the eastern coast of America. This colonisation, particularly by people who disagreed with the religious views of the next two kings, greatly increased in the next century.

The Elizabethan period is also remembered for the richness of its poetry and drama, especially the plays and poems of William Shakespeare (see next page).

James VI and I

Elizabeth I never married and so had no children of her own to inherit her throne. When she died in 1603 her heir was her cousin James VI of Scotland. He became King James I of England, Wales and Ireland but Scotland remained a separate country.

The King James Bible

One achievement of King James' reign was a new translation of the Bible into English. This translation is known as the 'King James Version' or the 'Authorised Version'. It was not the first English Bible but is a version which continues to be used in many Protestant churches today.

William Shakespeare (1564–1616)

Shakespeare was born in Stratford-upon-Avon, England. He was a playwright and actor and wrote many poems and plays. His most famous plays include *A Midsummer Night's Dream, Hamlet, Macbeth* and *Romeo and Juliet*. He also dramatised significant events from the past, but he did not focus solely on kings and queens. He was one of the first to portray ordinary Englishmen and women. Shakespeare had a great influence on the English language and invented many words that are still common today.

Lines from his plays and poems which are often still quoted include:
- Once more unto the breach (*Henry V*)
- To be or not to be (*Hamlet*)
- A rose by any other name (*Romeo and Juliet*)
- All the world's a stage (*As You Like It*)
- The darling buds of May (*Sonnet 18 – Shall I Compare Thee To a Summer's Day*).

Many people regard Shakespeare as the greatest playwright of all time. His plays and poems are still performed and studied in Britain and other countries today. The Globe Theatre in London is a modern copy of the theatres in which his plays were first performed.

Ireland

During this period, Ireland was an almost completely Catholic country. Henry VII and Henry VIII had extended English control outside the Pale (see War at Home and Abroad) and had established English authority over the whole country. Henry VIII took the title 'King of Ireland'. English laws were introduced and local leaders were expected to follow the instructions of the Lord Lieutenants in Dublin.

During the reigns of Elizabeth I and James I, many people in Ireland opposed rule by the Protestant government in England. There were a number of rebellions. The English government encouraged Scottish and English Protestants to settle in Ulster, the northern province of Ireland, taking over the land from Catholic landholders. These settlements were known as plantations. Many of the new settlers came from south-west Scotland and other land was given to companies based in London. James later organised similar plantations in several other parts of Ireland. This had serious long-term consequences for the history of England, Scotland and Ireland.

The rise of Parliament

Elizabeth I was very skilled at managing Parliament. During her reign, she was successful in balancing her wishes and views against those of the House of Lords and those of the House of Commons, which was increasingly Protestant in its views.

A long and illustrious history - 3. The Tudors and Stuarts

James I and his son Charles I were less skilled politically. Both believed in the 'Divine Right of Kings': the idea that the king was directly appointed by God to rule. They thought that the king should be able to act without having to seek approval from Parliament. When Charles I inherited the thrones of England, Wales, Ireland and Scotland, he tried to rule in line with this principle. When he could not get Parliament to agree with his religious and foreign policies, he tried to rule without Parliament at all. For 11 years, he found ways in which to raise money without Parliament's approval but eventually trouble in Scotland meant that he had to recall Parliament.

The beginning of the English civil war

Charles I wanted the worship of the Church of England to include more ceremony and introduced a revised Prayer Book. He tried to impose this Prayer Book on the Presbyterian Church in Scotland and this led to serious unrest. A Scottish army was formed and Charles could not find the money he needed for his own army without the help of Parliament. In 1640, he recalled Parliament to ask it for funds. Many in Parliament were Puritans, a group of Protestants who advocated strict and simple religious doctrine and worship. They did not agree with the king's religious views and disliked his reforms of the Church of England. Parliament refused to give the king the money he asked for, even after the Scottish army invaded England.

Charles I believed in his Divine Right to rule and oppsed Parliament.

Another rebellion began in Ireland because the Roman Catholics in Ireland were afraid of the growing power of the Puritans. Parliament took this opportunity to demand control of the English army – a change that would have transferred substantial power from the king to Parliament. In response, Charles I entered the House of Commons and tried to arrest five parliamentary leaders, but they had been warned and were not there. (No monarch has set foot in the Commons since.) Civil war between the king and Parliament could not now be avoided and began in 1642. The country split into those who supported the king (the Cavaliers) and those who supported Parliament (the Roundheads).

Charles I is the last Monarch to enter House of Commons.

Oliver Cromwell and the English Republic

The king's army was defeated at the Battles of Marston Moor and Naseby. By 1646, it was clear that Parliament had won the war. Charles was held prisoner by the parliamentary army. He was still unwilling to reach any agreement with Parliament and in 1649 he was executed.

England declared itself a republic, called the Commonwealth. It no longer had a monarch. For a time, it was not totally clear how the country would be governed. For now, the army was in control. One of its generals, Oliver Cromwell, was sent to Ireland, where the revolt which had begun in 1641 still continued and where there was still a Royalist army. Cromwell was successful in establishing the authority of the English Parliament but did this with such violence that even today Cromwell remains a controversial figure in Ireland.

The Scots had not agreed to the execution of Charles I and declared his son Charles II to be king. He was crowned king of Scotland and led a Scottish army into England. Cromwell defeated this army in the Battles of Dunbar and Worcester. Charles II escaped from Worcester, famously hiding in an oak tree on one occasion, and eventually fled to Europe. Parliament now controlled Scotland as well as England and Wales.

After his campaign in Ireland and victory over Charles II at Worcester, Cromwell was recognised as the leader of the new republic. He was given the title of Lord Protector and ruled until his death in 1658. When Cromwell died, his son, Richard, became Lord Protector in his place but was not able to control the army or the government. Although Britain had been a republic for 11 years, without Oliver Cromwell there was no clear leader or system of government. Many people in the country wanted stability. People began to talk about the need for a king.

> For 11 years, England was a republic.

The Restoration
In May 1660, Parliament invited Charles II to come back from exile in the Netherlands. He was crowned King Charles II of England, Wales, Scotland and Ireland. Charles II made it clear that he had 'no wish to go on his travels again'. He understood that he could not always do as he wished but would sometimes need to reach agreement with Parliament. Generally, Parliament supported his policies. The Church of England again became the established official Church. Both Roman Catholics and Puritans were kept out of power.

St Pauls - Mark Fosh

During Charles II's reign, in 1665, there was a major outbreak of plague in London. Thousands of people died, especially in poorer areas. The following year, a great fire destroyed much of the city, including many churches and St Paul's Cathedral. London was rebuilt with a new St Paul's, which was designed by a famous architect, Sir Christopher Wren. Samuel Pepys wrote about these events in a diary which was later published and is still read today.

The Habeas Corpus Act became law in 1679. This was a very important piece of legislation which remains relevant today. Habeas corpus is Latin for 'you must present the person in court'. The Act guaranteed that no one could be held prisoner unlawfully. Every prisoner has a right to a court hearing.

> The Habeas Corpus of 1679 protects against unlawful imprisonment.

Isaac Newton - Godfrey Kneller

Charles II was interested in science. During his reign, the Royal Society was formed to promote 'natural knowledge'. This is the oldest surviving scientific society in the world. Among its early members were Sir Edmund Halley, who successfully predicted the return of the comet now called Halley's Comet, and Sir Isaac Newton.

A long and illustrious history - 3. The Tudors and Stuarts

Isaac Newton (1643–1727)

Born in Lincolnshire, eastern England, Isaac Newton first became interested in science when he studied at Cambridge University. He became an important figure in the field. His most famous published work was Philosophiae Naturalis Principia Mathematica (*'Mathematical Principles of Natural Philosophy'*), which showed how gravity applied to the whole universe. Newton also discovered that white light is made up of the colours of the rainbow. Many of his discoveries are still important for modern science.

A Catholic King

Charles II had no legitimate children. He died in 1685 and his brother, James, who was a Roman Catholic, became King James II in England, Wales and Ireland and King James VII of Scotland. James favoured Roman Catholics and allowed them to be army Officers, which an Act of Parliament had forbidden. He did not seek to reach agreements with Parliament and arrested some of the bishops of the Church of England. People in England worried that James wanted to make England a Catholic country once more. However, his heirs were his two daughters, who were both firmly Protestant, and people thought that this meant there would soon be a Protestant monarch again. Then, James's wife had a son. Suddenly, it seemed likely that the next monarch would not be a Protestant after all.

The Glorious Revolution

James II's elder daughter, Mary, was married to her cousin William of Orange, the Protestant ruler of the Netherlands. In 1688, important Protestants in England asked William to invade England and proclaim himself king.

The Glorious Revolution was a peacefull transition of power.

When William reached England, there was no resistance. James fled to France and William took over the throne, becoming William III in England, Wales and Ireland, and William II of Scotland. William ruled jointly with Mary. This event was later called the 'Glorious Revolution' because there was no fighting in England and because it guaranteed the power of Parliament, ending the threat of a monarch ruling on his or her own as he or she wished.

William of Orange III and his Dutch army land in Brixham by Hoynck van Papendrecht, J.

James II wanted to regain the throne and invaded Ireland with the help of a French army. William defeated James II at the Battle of the Boyne in Ireland in 1690, an event which is still celebrated by some in Northern Ireland today. William re-conquered Ireland and James fled back to France. Many restrictions were placed on the Roman Catholic Church in Ireland and Irish Catholics were unable to take part in the government.

There was also support for James in Scotland. An attempt at an armed rebellion in support of James was quickly defeated at Killiecrankie. All Scottish clans were required formally to accept William as king by taking an oath. The MacDonalds of Glencoe were late in taking the oath and were all killed. The memory of this massacre meant some Scots distrusted the new government.

Some continued to believe that James was the rightful king, particularly in Scotland. Some joined him in exile in France; others were secret supporters. James' supporters became known as Jacobites.

Key points to remember
- Henry VIII breaks away from the Church of Rome and marry 6 women.
- Protestantism grows stronger in England as a reform against the Catholic Church, but leads to conflicts, most especially in Ireland that remains very Catholic.
- Queen Elizabeth I, daughter of Henry VIII, brings appeasement to years of religious fights but keep her own cousin Queen Mary prisoner for 20 years.
- The Elizabethan period sees an increase in maritime exploration which leads to the expansion of British trade abroad, often against the Spanish. Conflicts with Spain are frequent and culminate with the defeat of the Spanish Armada in 1588.
- The period also witnesses a cultural revival notably with Shakespeare.
- Tensions with Parliament reignites after Queen Elizabeth's death. Charles I opposes his Divine Right to rule to shared power. This leads to a civil war in 1648 until the king is defeated and executed in 1649.
- Oliver Cromwell, an army general, re-establishes Parliament's authority in Ireland and England and becomes Lord Protector in 1658.
- For 11 years, England is a republic.
- The Restoration starts in 1660 with the return of Charles II from exile.
- London is hit by the Plague in 1665 and a great fire in 1666.
- For 2 centuries, England swings between Catholics and Protestants.
- During the Glorious Revolution of 1688, prominent Protestants invite William of Orange from the Netherlands to become King. There's no resistance.

4. A global power

Constitutional monarchy – The Bill of Rights

At the coronation of William and Mary, a Declaration of Rights was read. This confirmed that the king would no longer be able to raise taxes or administer justice without agreement from Parliament. The balance of power between monarch and Parliament had now permanently changed. The Bill of Rights, 1689, confirmed the rights of Parliament and the limits of the king's power. Parliament took control of who could be monarch and declared that the king or queen must be a Protestant. A new Parliament had to be elected at least every three years (later this became seven years and now it is five years). Every year the monarch had to ask Parliament to renew funding for the army and the navy.

The first 2 political parties in Parliament were the Tories and the Whigs.

These changes meant that, to be able to govern effectively, the monarch needed to have advisers, or ministers, who would be able to ensure a majority of votes in the House of Commons and the House of Lords. There were two main groups in Parliament, known as the Whigs and the Tories. (The modern Conservative Party is still sometimes referred to as the Tories.) This was the beginning of party politics.

This was also an important time for the development of a free press (newspapers and other publications which are not controlled by the government). From 1695, newspapers were allowed to operate without a government licence. Increasing numbers of newspapers began to be published.

The laws passed after the Glorious Revolution are the beginning of what is called 'constitutional monarchy'. The monarch remained very important but was no longer able to insist on particular policies or actions if Parliament did not agree. After William III, the ministers gradually became more important than the monarch but this was not a democracy in the modern sense. The number of people who had the right to vote for members of Parliament was still very small. Only men who owned property of a certain value were able to vote. No women at all had the vote. Some constituencies were controlled by a single wealthy family. These were called 'pocket boroughs'. Other constituencies had hardly any voters and were called 'rotten boroughs'.

Pocket Boroughs
Parliamentary borough where potentially a single man or family can control the vote.

Rotten Boroughs
Parliamentary borough with very small electorate. for instance, where population has declined.

A growing population
This was a time when many people left Britain and Ireland to settle in new colonies in America and elsewhere, but others came to live in Britain. The first Jews to come to Britain since the Middle Ages settled in London in 1656. Between 1680 and 1720 many refugees called Huguenots came from France. They were Protestants and had been persecuted for their religion. Many were educated and skilled and worked as scientists, in banking, or in weaving or other crafts.

Huguenots were Protestants refugees from France.

The Act of Treaty or Union in Scotland
William and Mary's successor, Queen Anne, had no surviving children. This created uncertainty over the succession in England, Wales and Ireland and in Scotland. The Act of Union, known as the Treaty of Union in Scotland, was therefore agreed in 1707, creating the Kingdom of Great Britain. Although Scotland was no longer an independent country, it kept its own legal and education systems and Presbyterian Church.

The Prime Minister
When Queen Anne died in 1714, Parliament chose a German, George I, to be the next king, because he was Anne's nearest Protestant relative. An attempt by Scottish Jacobites to put James II's son on the throne instead was quickly defeated. George I did not speak very good English and this increased his need to rely on his ministers. The most important minister in Parliament became known as the Prime Minister. The first man to be called this was Sir Robert Walpole, who was Prime Minister from 1721 to 1742.

Sir Robert Walpole became the first Prime Minister.

The rebellion of the clans

In 1745 there was another attempt to put a Stuart king back on the throne in place of George I's son, George II. Charles Edward Stuart (Bonnie Prince Charlie), the grandson of James II, landed in Scotland. He was supported by clansmen from the Scottish highlands and raised an army. Charles initially had some successes but was defeated by George II's army at the Battle of Culloden in 1746. Charles escaped back to Europe.

The clans lost a lot of their power and influence after Culloden. Chieftains became landlords if they had the favour of the English king, and clansmen became tenants who had to pay for the land they used.

A process began which became known as the 'Highland Clearances'. Many Scottish landlords destroyed individual small farms (known as 'crofts') to make space for large flocks of sheep and cattle. Evictions became very common in the early 19th century. Many Scottish people left for North America at this time.

> **Robert Burns (1759–96)**
> Known in Scotland as 'The Bard', Robert Burns was a Scottish poet. He wrote in the Scots language, English with some Scottish words, and standard English. He also revised a lot of traditional folk songs by changing or adding lyrics. Burns' best-known work is probably the song *Auld Lang Syne*, which is sung by people in the UK and other countries when they are celebrating the New Year (or Hogmanay in Scotland).

The Enlightenment

During the 18th century, new ideas about politics, philosophy and science were developed. This is often called 'the Enlightenment'. Many of the great thinkers of the Enlightenment were Scottish. Adam Smith developed ideas about economics which are still referred to today. David Hume's ideas about human nature continue to influence philosophers. Scientific discoveries, such as James Watt's work on steam power, helped the progress of the Industrial Revolution.

One of the most important principles of the Enlightenment was that everyone should have the right to their own political and religious beliefs and that the state should not try to dictate to them. This continues to be an important principle in the UK today.

The Industrial Revolution

Before the 18th century, agriculture was the biggest source of employment in Britain. There were many cottage industries, where people worked from home to produce goods such as cloth and lace.

The Industrial Revolution was the rapid development of industry in Britain in the 18th and 19th centuries. Britain was

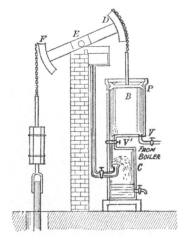

Watt steam engine from practical physics for secondary schools. fundamental principles and applications to daily life, publ. 1913

the first country to industrialise on a large scale. It happened because of the development of machinery and the use of steam power. Agriculture and the manufacturing of goods became mechanised. This made things more efficient and increased production. Coal and other raw materials were needed to power the new factories. Many people moved from the countryside and started working in the mining and manufacturing industries.

The development of the Bessemer process for the mass production of steel led to the development of the shipbuilding industry and the railways. Manufacturing jobs became the main source of employment in Britain.

Richard Arkwright (1732–92)
Born in 1732, Arkwright originally trained and worked as a barber. He was able to dye hair and make wigs. When wigs became less popular, he started to work in textiles. He improved the original carding machine. Carding is the process of preparing fibres for spinning into yarn and fabric. He also developed horse-driven spinning mills that used only one machine. This increased the efficiency of production. Later, he used the steam engine to power machinery. Arkwright is particularly remembered for the efficient and profitable way that he ran his factories.

Better transport links were needed to transport raw materials and manufactured goods. Canals were built to link the factories to towns and cities and to the ports, particularly in the new industrial areas in the middle and north of England.

Working conditions during the Industrial Revolution were very poor. There were no laws to protect employees, who were often forced to work long hours in dangerous situations. Children also worked and were treated in the same way as adults. Sometimes they were treated even more harshly.

This was also a time of increased colonisation overseas. Captain James Cook mapped the coast of Australia and a few colonies were established there. Britain gained control over Canada, and the East India Company, originally set up to trade, gained control of large parts of India. Colonies began to be established in southern Africa.

Britain traded all over the world and began to import more goods. Sugar and tobacco came from North America and the West Indies; textiles, tea and spices came from India and the area that is today called Indonesia. Trading and settlements overseas sometimes brought Britain into conflict with other countries, particularly France, which was expanding and trading in a similar way in many of the same areas of the world.

Sake Dean Mahomet (1759–1851)
Mahomet was born in 1759 and grew up in the Bengal region of India. He served in the Bengal army and came to Britain in 1782. He then moved to Ireland and eloped with an Irish girl called Jane Daly in 1786, returning to England at the turn of the century. In 1810 he opened the Hindoostane Coffee House in George Street, London. It was the first curry house to open in Britain. Mahomet and his wife also introduced 'shampooing', the Indian art of head massage, to Britain.

The slave trade

This commercial expansion and prosperity was sustained in part by the booming slave trade. While slavery was illegal within Britain itself, by the 18th century it was a fully established overseas industry, dominated by Britain and the American colonies. Slaves came primarily from West Africa. Travelling on British ships in horrible conditions, they were taken to America and the Caribbean, where they were made to work on tobacco and sugar plantations. The living and working conditions for slaves were very bad. Many slaves tried to escape and others revolted against their owners in protest at their terrible treatment.

There were, however, people in Britain who opposed the slave trade. The first formal anti-slavery groups were set up by the Quakers in the late 1700s, and they petitioned Parliament to ban the practice. William Wilberforce, an evangelical Christian and a Member of Parliament, also played an important part in changing the law. Along with other abolitionists (people who supported the abolition of slavery), he succeeded in turning public opinion against the slave trade. In 1807, it became illegal to trade slaves in British ships or from British ports, and in 1833 the Emancipation Act abolished slavery throughout the British Empire. The Royal Navy stopped slave ships from other countries, freed the slaves and punished the slave traders. After 1833, 2 million Indian and Chinese workers were employed to replace the freed slaves. They worked on sugar plantations in the Caribbean, in mines in South Africa, on railways in East Africa and in the army in Kenya.

Slave trade became illegal in 1807 and slavery was abolished in 1833.

The American war of independence

By the 1760s, there were substantial British colonies in North America. The colonies were wealthy and largely in control of their own affairs. Many of the colonist families had originally gone to North America in order to have religious freedom. They were well educated and interested in ideas of liberty. The British government wanted to tax the colonies. The colonists saw this as an attack on their freedom and said there should be 'no taxation without representation' in the British Parliament. Parliament tried to compromise by repealing some of the taxes, but relationships between the British government and the colonies continued to worsen.

Declaration of Independence
US Library of Congress

Fighting broke out between the colonists and the British forces. In 1776, 13 American colonies declared their independence, stating that people had a right to establish their own governments. The colonists eventually defeated the British army and Britain recognised the colonies' independence in 1783.

War with France

During the 18th century, Britain fought a number of wars with France. In 1789, there was a revolution in France and the new French government soon declared war on Britain. Napoleon, who became Emperor of France, continued the war. Britain's navy fought against combined French and Spanish fleets, winning the Battle of Trafalgar in 1805.

Admiral Nelson was in charge of the British fleet at Trafalgar and was killed in the battle. Nelson's Column in Trafalgar Square, London, is a monument to him. His ship, HMS Victory, can be visited in Portsmouth. The British army also fought against the French. In 1815, the French Wars ended with the defeat of the Emperor Napoleon by the Duke of Wellington at the Battle of Waterloo. Wellington was known as the Iron Duke and later became Prime Minister.

The Union Flag

Although Ireland had had the same monarch as England and Wales since Henry VIII, it had remained a separate country. In 1801, Ireland became unified with England, Scotland and Wales after the Act of Union of 1800. This created the United Kingdom of Great Britain and Ireland. One symbol of this union between England, Scotland, Wales and Ireland was a new version of the official flag, the Union Flag. This is often called the Union Jack. The flag combined crosses associated with England, Scotland and Ireland. It is still used today as the official flag of the UK.

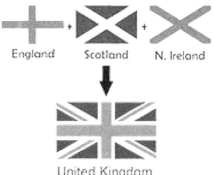

The Union Flag consists of three crosses:
- The cross of St George, patron saint of England, is a red cross on a white ground.
- The cross of St Andrew, patron saint of Scotland, is a diagonal white cross on a blue ground.
- The cross of St Patrick, patron saint of Ireland, is a diagonal red cross on a white ground.

There is also an official Welsh flag (left), which shows a Welsh dragon. The Welsh dragon does not appear on the Union Flag because, when the first Union Flag was created in 1606 from the flags of Scotland and England, the Principality of Wales was already united with England.

The Victorian Age

In 1837, Queen Victoria became queen of the UK at the age of 18. She reigned until 1901, almost 64 years. One of the longest reigning monarchs in the United Kingdom. Her reign is known as the Victorian Age. It was a time when Britain increased in power and influence abroad. Within the UK, the middle classes because increasingly significant and a number of reformers led moves to improve conditions of life for the poor.

The British Empire

During the Victorian period, the British Empire grew to cover all of India, Australia and large parts of Africa. It became the largest empire the world has ever seen, with an estimated population of more than 400 million people.

Many people were encouraged to leave the UK to settle overseas. Between 1853 and 1913, as many as 13 million British citizens left the country. People continued to come to Britain from other parts of the world. For example, between 1870 and 1914, around 120,000 Russian and Polish Jews came to Britain to escape persecution. Many settled in London's

East End and in Manchester and Leeds. People from the Empire, including India and Africa, also came to Britain to live, work and study.

Trade and industry

Britain continued to be a great trading nation. The government began to promote policies of free trade, abolishing a number of taxes on imported goods. One example of this was the repealing of the Corn Laws in 1846. These had prevented the import of cheap grain. The reforms helped the development of British industry, because raw materials could now be imported more cheaply.

Working conditions in factories gradually became better. In 1847, the number of hours that women and children could work was limited by law to 10 hours per day. Better housing began to be built for workers.

Transport links also improved, enabling goods and people to move more easily around the country. Just before Victoria came to the throne, the father and son George and Robert Stephenson pioneered the railway engine and a major expansion of the railways took place in the Victorian period. Railways were built throughout the Empire. There were also great advances in other areas, such as the building of bridges by engineers such as Isambard Kingdom Brunel.

Stephenson's Rocket- replica
Photo: Tony Hisgett from Birmingham,

Clifton Suspension Bridge designed by I.K. Brunel - Photo: Nic Trott

British industry led the world in the 19th century. The UK produced more than half of the world's iron, coal and cotton cloth. The UK also became a centre for financial services, including insurance and banking. In 1851, the Great Exhibition opened in Hyde Park in the Crystal Palace, a huge building made of steel and glass. Exhibits ranged from huge machines to handmade goods. Countries from all over the world showed their goods but most of the objects were made in Britain.

Isambard Kingdom Brunel (1806–59)
Brunel was originally from Portsmouth, England. He was an engineer who built tunnels, bridges, railway lines and ships. He was responsible for constructing the Great Western Railway, which was the first major railway built in Britain. It runs from Paddington Station in London to the south west of England, the West Midlands and Wales. Many of Brunel's bridges are still in use today.

The Crimean War

From 1853 to 1856, Britain fought with Turkey and France against Russia in the Crimean War. It was the first war to be extensively covered by the media through news stories and photographs. The conditions were very poor and many soldiers died from illnesses they caught in the hospitals, rather than from war wounds. Queen Victoria introduced the Victoria Cross medal (right) during this war. It honours acts of valour by soldiers.

Florence Nightingale (1820–1910)

Florence Nightingale was born in Italy to English parents. At the age of 31, she trained as a nurse in Germany. In 1854, she went to Turkey and worked in military hospitals, treating soldiers who were fighting in the Crimean War. She and her fellow nurses improved the conditions in the hospital and reduced the mortality rate. In 1860 she established the Nightingale Training School for nurses at St Thomas' Hospital in London. The school was the first of its kind and still exists today, as do many of the practices that Florence used. She is often regarded as the founder of modern nursing.

Ireland in the 19th century

Conditions in Ireland were not as good as in the rest of the UK. Two-thirds of the population still depended on farming to make their living, often on very small plots of land. Many depended on potatoes as a large part of their diet. In the middle of the century the potato crop failed, and Ireland suffered a famine. A million people died from disease and starvation. Another million and a half left Ireland. Some emigrated to the United States and others came to England. By 1861 there were large populations of Irish people in cities such as Liverpool, London, Manchester and Glasgow.

The Irish Nationalist movement had grown strongly through the 19th century. Some, such as the Fenians, favoured complete independence. Others, such as Charles Stuart Parnell, advocated 'Home Rule', in which Ireland would remain in the UK but have its own parliament.

The right to vote

As the middle classes in the wealthy industrial towns and cities grew in influence, they began to demand more political power. The Reform Act of 1832 had greatly increased the number of people with the right to vote. The Act also abolished the old pocket and rotten boroughs (see Constitutional Monarchy – The Bill of Rights p.25) and more parliamentary seats were given to the towns and cities. There was a permanent shift of political power from the countryside to the towns but voting was still based on ownership of property. This meant that members of the working class were still unable to vote.

A movement began to demand the vote for the working classes and other people without property. Campaigners, called the Chartists, presented petitions to Parliament. At first they seemed to be unsuccessful, but in 1867 there was another Reform Act. This created many more urban seats in Parliament and reduced the amount of property that people needed to have before they could vote. However, the majority of men still did not have the right to vote and no women could vote.

The Chartist campaigned from 1836 for workers right to vote, a salary for MPs, secret ballot, general elections and abolition of the need to own property.

Politicians realised that the increased number of voters meant that they needed to persuade people to vote for them if they were to be sure of being elected to Parliament. The political parties began to create organisations to reach out to ordinary voters. Universal suffrage (the right of every adult, male or female, to vote) followed in the next century.

In common with the rest of Europe, women in 19th century Britain had fewer rights than men. Until 1870, when a woman got married, her earnings, property and money automatically belonged to her husband. Acts of Parliament in 1870 and 1882 gave wives the right to keep their own earnings and property. In the late 19th and early 20th centuries, an increasing number of women campaigned and demonstrated for greater rights and, in particular, the right to vote. They formed the women's suffrage movement and became known as 'suffragettes'.

Emmeline Pankhurst addresses crowd
Topical Press Agency, Public Domain

Emmeline Pankhurst (1858–1928)
Emmeline Pankhurst was born in Manchester in 1858. She set up the Women's Franchise League in 1889, which fought to get the vote in local elections for married women. In 1903 she helped found the Women's Social and Political Union (WSPU). This was the first group whose members were called 'suffragettes'. The group used civil disobedience as part of their protest to gain the vote for women. They chained themselves to railings, smashed windows and committed arson. Many of the women, including Emmeline, went on hunger strike. In 1918, women over the age of 30 were given voting rights and the right to stand for Parliament, partly in recognition of the contribution women made to the war effort during the First World War. Shortly before Emmeline's death in 1928, women were given the right to vote at the age of 21, the same as men.

The future of the Empire

Although the British Empire continued to grow until the 1920s, there was already discussion in the late 19th century about its future direction. Supporters of expansion believed that the Empire benefited Britain through increased trade and commerce. Others thought the Empire had become over-expanded and that the frequent conflicts in many parts of the Empire, such as India's north-west frontier or southern Africa, were a drain on resources. Yet the great majority of British people believed in the Empire as a force for good in the world.

The Boer War of 1899 to 1902 made the discussions about the future of the Empire more urgent. The British went to war in South Africa with settlers from the Netherlands called the Boers. The Boers fought fiercely and the war went on for over three years. Many died in the fighting and many more from disease. There was some public

The Boer War in South Africa (1899-1902) saw the start of a strong demand for independence by parts of the British empire.

sympathy for the Boers and people began to question whether the Empire could continue. As different parts of the Empire developed, they won greater freedom and autonomy from Britain. Eventually, by the second half of the 20th century, there was, for the most part, an orderly transition from Empire to Commonwealth, with countries being granted their independence.

Rudyard Kipling (1865–1936)
Rudyard Kipling was born in India in 1865 and later lived in India, the UK and the USA. He wrote books and poems set in both India and the UK. His poems and novels reflected the idea that the British Empire was a force for good. Kipling was awarded the Nobel Prize in Literature in 1907. His books include the Just So Stories and The Jungle Book, which continue to be popular today. His poem *If* has often been voted among the UK's favourite poems. It begins with these words:

'If you can keep your head when all about you
Are losing theirs and blaming it on you;
If you can trust yourself when all men doubt you,
But make allowance for their doubting too;
If you can wait and not be tired by waiting,
Or being lied about, don't deal in lies,
Or being hated, don't give way to hating,
And yet don't look too good, nor talk too wise'

Key points to remember:
- The Bill of Rights of 1689 crystallises the respective powers of Parliament and the Monarch. The constitutional monarchy is established, and politics start.
- Queen Anne signs the Acts of Union in 1707 and creates the Kingdom of Great Britain, uniting England, Scotland and Wales but peace is not straightforward.
- A new role appears in 1729, that of Prime Minister.
- The Enlightenment during the 18th century brings new societal and political ideas and drives the development of free press.
- Progress in science leads to vast industrial developments in the 18th century.
- Many leave the farms to work in factory and mines but conditions are not good.
- The British Empire expands through colonisation and slave trade.
- An increase in taxes for colonies lead to some in North American to rebel. Fighting leads to war and in 1776, 13 colonies declare their independence.
- The French revolution of 1789 leads to war with England which continues until Napoleon is defeated at Waterloo in 1815 by the Duke of Wellington.
- The union with Ireland in 1881 creates the United Kingdom. A new flag is formed: the Union Jack.
- At 18, Victoria becomes Queen. She'll reign for 64 years until 1901 and will oversee the largest growth of the Empire.
- During the Victorian era, trade, travel and industry develops fast.
- The middle class grows and soon demands an increased political role. Vote rights increase first with the Chartists and then the Suffragettes.
- After the Boer war in 1899, other countries seek to leave the British Empire.

5. The 20th century

The First World War

The early 20th century was a time of optimism in Britain. The nation, with its expansive Empire, well-admired navy, thriving industry and strong political institutions, was what is now known as a global 'superpower'. It was also a time of social progress. Financial help for the unemployed, old-age pensions and free school meals were just a few of the important measures introduced. Various laws were passed to improve safety in the workplace; town planning rules were tightened to prevent the further development of slums; and better support was given to mothers and their children after divorce or separation. Local government became more democratic and a salary for members of Parliament (MPs) was introduced for the first time, making it easier for more people to take part in public life.

This era of optimism and progress was cut short when war broke out between several European nations. On 28 June 1914, Archduke Franz Ferdinand of Austria was assassinated. This set off a chain of events leading to the First World War (1914–18). But while the assassination provided the trigger for war, other factors – such as a growing sense of nationalism in many European states; increasing militarism; imperialism; and the division of the major European powers into two camps – all set the conditions for war.

The conflict was centred in Europe, but it was a global war involving nations from around the world. Britain was part of the Allied Powers, which included (amongst others) France, Russia, Japan, Belgium, Serbia – and later, Greece, Italy, Romania and the United States. The whole of the British Empire was involved in the conflict – for example, more than a million Indians fought on behalf of Britain in lots of different countries, and around 40,000 were killed. Men from the West Indies, Africa, Australia, New Zealand and Canada also fought with the British.

The assassination of Archduke Franz Ferdinand of Austria in June 1914 triggers World War I.

The Allies fought against the Central Powers – mainly Germany, the Austro-Hungarian Empire, the Ottoman Empire and later Bulgaria. Millions of people were killed or wounded, with more than 2 million British casualties. One battle, the British attack on the Somme in July 1916, resulted in about 60,000 British casualties on the first day alone.

The First World War ended at 11.00 am on 11th November 1918 with victory for Britain and its allies.

The partition of Ireland

In 1913, the British government promised 'Home Rule' for Ireland. The proposal was to have a self-governing Ireland with its own parliament but still part of the UK. A Home Rule Bill was introduced in Parliament. It was opposed by the Protestants in the north of Ireland, who threatened to resist Home Rule by force.

The outbreak of the First World War led the British government to postpone any changes in Ireland. Irish Nationalists were not willing to wait and in 1916 there was an uprising (the Easter Rising) against the British in Dublin. The leaders of the uprising were executed under military law. A guerrilla war against the British army and the police in Ireland followed. In 1921 a peace treaty was signed and in 1922 Ireland became two countries. The six counties in the north which were mainly Protestant remained part of the UK under the name Northern Ireland. The rest of Ireland became the Irish Free State. It had its own government and became a republic in 1949 (see map).

There were people in both parts of Ireland who disagreed with the split between the North and the South. They still wanted Ireland to be one independent country. Years of disagreement led to a terror campaign in Northern Ireland and elsewhere. The conflict between those wishing for full Irish independence and those wishing to remain loyal to the British government is often referred to as 'the Troubles'.

The inter-war period

In the 1920s, many people's living conditions got better. There were improvements in public housing and new homes were built in many towns and cities. However, in 1929, the world entered the 'Great Depression' and some parts of the UK suffered mass unemployment. The effects of the depression of the 1930s were felt differently in different parts of the UK. The traditional heavy industries such as shipbuilding were badly affected but new industries – including the automobile and aviation industries – developed. As prices generally fell, those in work had more money to spend. Car ownership doubled from 1 million to 2 million between 1930 and 1939. In addition, many new houses were built. It was also a time of cultural blossoming, with writers such as Graham Greene and Evelyn Waugh prominent. The economist John Maynard Keynes published influential new theories of economics. The BBC started radio broadcasts in 1922 and began the world's first regular television service in 1936.

The Second World War

Adolf Hitler came to power in Germany in 1933. He believed that the conditions imposed on Germany by the Allies after the First World War were unfair; he also wanted to conquer more land for the German people. He set about renegotiating treaties, building up arms, and testing Germany's military strength in nearby countries. The British government tried to avoid another war. However, when Hitler invaded Poland in 1939, Britain and France declared war in order to stop his aggression.

The war was initially fought between the Axis powers (fascist Germany and Italy and the Empire of Japan) and the Allies. The main countries on the allied side were the UK, France, Poland, Australia, New Zealand, Canada, and the Union of South Africa.

Having occupied Austria and invaded Czechoslovakia, Hitler followed his invasion of Poland by taking control of Belgium and the Netherlands. Then, in 1940, German forces defeated allied troops and advanced through France. At this time of national crisis, Winston Churchill became Prime Minister and Britain's war leader.

As France fell, the British decided to evacuate British and French soldiers from France in a huge naval operation. Many civilian volunteers in small pleasure and fishing boats from Britain helped the Navy to rescue more than 300,000 men from the beaches around Dunkirk. Although many lives and a lot of equipment were lost, the evacuation was a success and meant that Britain was better able to continue the fight against the Germans. The evacuation gave rise to the phrase 'the Dunkirk spirit'.

From the end of June 1940 until the German invasion of the Soviet Union in June 1941, Britain and the Empire stood almost alone against Nazi Germany.

Hitler wanted to invade Britain, but before sending in troops, Germany needed to control the air. The Germans waged an air campaign against Britain, but the British resisted with their fighter planes and eventually won the crucial aerial battle against the Germans, called 'the Battle of Britain', in the summer of 1940. The most important planes used by the Royal Air Force in the Battle of Britain were the Spitfire and the Hurricane – which were designed and built in Britain. Despite this crucial victory, the German air force was able to continue bombing London and other British cities at night-time. This was called the Blitz. Coventry was almost totally destroyed and a great deal of damage was done in other cities, especially in the East End of London. Despite the destruction, there was a strong national spirit of resistance in the UK. The phrase 'the Blitz spirit' is still used today to describe Britons pulling together in the face of adversity.

Allied Powers		Axis Powers
The UK, The US, France, Poland, Australia, New Zealand, Canada, the Union of South Africa, Russia and many others.	**fought against**	mainly Nazi Germany, Italy and the Empire of Japan. Also Bulgaria, Croatia, Hungary, Romania, and Slovakia.

At the same time as defending Britain, the British military was fighting the Axis on many other fronts. In Singapore, the Japanese defeated the British and then occupied Burma, threatening India. The United States entered the war when the Japanese bombed its naval base at Pearl Harbour in December 1941.

That same year, Hitler attempted the largest invasion in history by attacking the Soviet Union. It was a fierce conflict, with huge losses on both sides. German forces were ultimately repelled by the Soviets, and the damage they sustained proved to be a pivotal point in the war.

The allied forces gradually gained the upper hand, winning significant victories in North Africa and Italy. German losses in the Soviet Union, combined with the support of the Americans, meant that the Allies were eventually strong enough to attack Hitler's forces in Western Europe. On 6 June 1944, allied forces landed in Normandy (this event is often referred to as 'D-Day'). Following victory on the beaches of Normandy, the allied forces pressed on through France and eventually into Germany. The Allies comprehensively defeated Germany in May 1945.

Winston Churchill (1874–1965)

Churchill was the son of a politician and, before becoming a Conservative MP in 1900, was a soldier and journalist. In May 1940 he became Prime Minister. He refused to surrender to the Nazis and was an inspirational leader to the British people in a time of great hardship. He lost the General Election in 1945 but returned as Prime Minister in 1951.

He was an MP until he stood down at the 1964 General Election. Following his death in 1965, he was given a state funeral. He remains a much-admired figure to this day, and in 2002 was voted the greatest Briton of all time by the public. During the War, he made many famous speeches including lines which you may still hear:

'I have nothing to offer but blood, toil, tears and sweat'
Churchill's first PM speech to the House of Commons, 1940

'We shall fight on the beaches,
we shall fight on the landing grounds,
we shall fight in the fields and in the streets,
we shall fight in the hills;
we shall never surrender'
Speech to the House of Commons after Dunkirk (see above), 1940

'Never in the field of human conflict was so much owed by so many to so few'
Speech to the House of Commons during the Battle of Britain, 1940

The war against Japan ended in August 1945 when the United States dropped its newly developed atom bombs on the Japanese cities of Hiroshima and Nagasaki. Scientists led by Ernest Rutherford, working at Manchester and then Cambridge University, were the first to 'split the atom' and took part in the Manhattan Project in the United States, which developed the atomic bomb. The war was finally over.

Key points to remember:
- The 20th century ushers a wave of optimism, abruptly stopped by World War I.
- The war pauses the process to give Ireland self-governing powers and in 1916, the Great Rising challenges British rule.
- A peace treaty is signed in 1921 and splits Ireland into 2 countries. Years of conflict would ensue, often referred to as The Troubles.
- World War II starts in 1939, after Nazi Germany invades Poland.
- Churchill becomes Prime minister after the defeat of 1940 in Dunkirk.
- Britain defends itself against Nazi invasion in 1940 during the Battle for Britain.
- The US join the war in 1941 after the Japanese attack in Pearl Harbour.
- The allied forces land in Normandy, France on 6th June 1944 and repel the German troops throughout Western Europe while the Russians push them back across Eastern Europe.
- The Nazis are defeated in Europe in May 1945 and the war ends after Japan surrender in August 1945.

6. Britain since 1945

The welfare state

Although the UK had won the war, the country was exhausted economically and the people wanted change. During the war, there had been significant reforms to the education system and people now looked for wider social reforms.

In 1945 the British people elected a Labour government. The new Prime Minister was Clement Atlee, who promised to introduce the welfare state outlined in the Beveridge Report. In 1948, Aneurin (Nye) Bevan, the Minister for Health, led the establishment of the National Health Service (NHS), which guaranteed a minimum standard of health care for all, free at the point of use. A national system of benefits was also introduced to provide 'social security', so that the population would be protected from the 'cradle to the grave'. The government took into public ownership (nationalised) the railways, coal mines and gas, water and electricity supplies.

> **Alexander Fleming (1881–1955)**
> Born in Scotland, Fleming moved to London as a teenager and later qualified as a doctor. He was researching influenza (the 'flu') in 1928 when he discovered penicillin. This was then further developed into a usable drug by the scientists Howard Florey and Ernst Chain. By the 1940s it was in mass production. Fleming won the Nobel Prize in Medicine in 1945. Penicillin is still used to treat bacterial infections today.

Another aspect of change was self-government for former colonies. In 1947, independence was granted to nine countries, including India, Pakistan and Ceylon (now Sri Lanka). Other colonies in Africa, the Caribbean and the Pacific achieved independence over the next 20 years.

The UK developed its own atomic bomb and joined the new North Atlantic Treaty Organization (NATO), an alliance of nations set up to resist the perceived threat of invasion by the Soviet Union and its allies.

Britain had a Conservative government from 1951 to 1964. The 1950s were a period of economic recovery after the war and increasing prosperity for working people. The Prime Minister of the day, Harold Macmillan, was famous for his 'wind of change' speech about decolonisation and independence for the countries of the Empire.

> **William Beveridge (1879–1963)**
> William Beveridge (later Lord Beveridge) was a British economist and social reformer. He served briefly as a Liberal MP and was subsequently the leader of the Liberals in the House of Lords but is best known for the 1942 report Social Insurance and Allied Services (known as the Beveridge Report). The report was commissioned by the wartime government in 1941. It recommended that the government should find ways of fighting the five 'Giant Evils' of Want, Disease, Ignorance, Squalor and Idleness and provided the basis of the modern welfare state.

Clement Attlee (1883–1967)

Clement Attlee was born in London in 1883. His father was a solicitor and, after studying at Oxford University, Attlee became a barrister. He gave this up to do social work in East London and eventually became a Labour MP. He was Winston Churchill's Deputy Prime Minister in the wartime coalition government and became Prime Minister after the Labour Party won the 1945 election. He was Prime Minister from 1945 to 1951 and led the Labour Party for 20 years. Attlee's government undertook the nationalisation of major industries (like coal and steel), created the National Health Service and implemented many of Beveridge's plans for a stronger welfare state. Attlee also introduced measures to improve the conditions of workers.

R A Butler (1902–82)

Richard Austen Butler (later Lord Butler) was born in 1902. He became a Conservative MP in 1923 and held several positions before becoming responsible for education in 1941. In this role, he oversaw the introduction of the Education Act 1944 (often called 'The Butler Act'), which introduced free secondary education in England and Wales. The education system has changed significantly since the Act was introduced, but the division between primary and secondary schools that it enforced still remains in most areas of Britain.

Dylan Thomas (1914–53)

Dylan Thomas was a Welsh poet and writer. He often read and performed his work in public, including for the BBC. His most well-known works include the radio play Under Milk Wood, first performed after his death in 1954, and the poem Do Not Go Gentle into That Good Night, which he wrote for his dying father in 1952. He died at the age of 39 in New York. There are several memorials to him in his birthplace, Swansea, including a statue and the Dylan Thomas Centre.

Migration in post-war Britain

Rebuilding Britain after the Second World War was a huge task. There were labour shortages and the British government encouraged workers from Ireland and other parts of Europe to come to the UK and help with the reconstruction. In 1948, people from the West Indies were also invited to come and work.

During the 1950s, there was still a shortage of labour in the UK. Further immigration was therefore encouraged for economic reasons, and many industries advertised for workers from overseas. For example, centres were set up in the West Indies to recruit people to drive buses. Textile and engineering firms from the north of England and the Midlands sent agents to India and Pakistan to find workers. For about 25 years, people from the West Indies, India, Pakistan and (later) Bangladesh travelled to work and settle in Britain.

Social change in the 1960s

The decade of the 1960s was a period of significant social change. It was known as 'the Swinging Sixties'. There was growth in British fashion, cinema and popular music. Two well-known pop music groups at the time were The Beatles and The Rolling Stones. People started to become better off and many bought cars and other consumer goods.

It was also a time when social laws were liberalised, for example in relation to divorce and to abortion in England, Wales and Scotland. The position of women in the workplace also improved. It was quite common at the time for employers to ask women to leave their jobs when they got married, but Parliament passed new laws giving women the right to equal pay and made it illegal for employers to discriminate against women because of their gender.

The 1960s was also a time of technological progress. Britain and France developed the world's only supersonic commercial airliner, Concorde. New styles of architecture, including high-rise buildings and the use of concrete and steel, became common.

Concorde - photo: Phillip Capper

The number of people migrating from the West Indies, India, Pakistan and what is now Bangladesh fell in the late 1960s because the government passed new laws to restrict immigration to Britain. Immigrants were required to have a strong connection to Britain through birth or ancestry. Even so, during the early 1970s, Britain admitted 28,000 people of Indian origin who had been forced to leave Uganda.

Some great British inventions of the 20th century
Britain has given the world some wonderful inventions. Examples from the 20th century include:
- The **television** was developed by Scotsman John Logie Baird (1888–1946) in the 1920s. In 1932 he made the first television broadcast between London and Glasgow.
- **Radar** was developed by Scotsman Sir Robert Watson-Watt (1892–1973), who proposed that enemy aircraft could be detected by radio waves. The first successful radar test took place in 1935.
- Working with radar led Sir Bernard Lovell (1913–2012) to make new discoveries in astronomy. The **radio telescope** he built at Jodrell Bank in Cheshire was for many years the biggest in the world and continues to operate today.
- A **Turing machine** is a theoretical mathematical device invented by Alan Turing (1912–54), a British mathematician, in the 1930s. The theory was influential in the development of computer science and the modern-day computer.
- The Scottish physician and researcher John MacLeod (1876–1935) was the co-discoverer of **insulin**, used to treat diabetes.
- The structure of the **DNA** molecule was discovered in 1953 through work at British universities in London and Cambridge. This discovery contributed to many scientific advances, particularly in medicine and fighting crime. Francis Crick (1916–2004), one of those awarded the Nobel Prize for this discovery, was British.
- The **jet engine** was developed in Britain in the 1930s by Sir Frank Whittle (1907–96), a British Royal Air Force engineer Officer.
- Sir Christopher Cockerell (1910–99), a British inventor, invented the **hovercraft** in the 1950s.
- Britain and France developed **Concorde**, the world's only supersonic passenger

aircraft. It first flew in 1969 and began carrying passengers in 1976. Concorde was retired from service in 2003.

- The **Harrier jump jet**, an aircraft capable of taking off vertically, was also designed and developed in the UK.
- In the 1960s, James Goodfellow (1937–) invented the **cash-dispensing ATM** (automatic teller machine) or 'cashpoint'. The first of these was put into use by Barclays Bank in Enfield, north London in 1967.
- **IVF (in-vitro fertilisation)** therapy for the treatment of infertility was pioneered in Britain by physiologist Sir Robert Edwards (1925–) and gynaecologist Patrick Steptoe (1913–88). The world's first 'test-tube baby' was born in Oldham, Lancashire in 1978.
- In 1996, two British scientists, Sir Ian Wilmot (1944–) and Keith Campbell (1954–2012), led a team which was the first to succeed in **cloning** a mammal, Dolly the sheep. This has led to further research into the possible use of cloning to preserve endangered species and for medical purposes.
- Sir Peter Mansfield (1933–), a British scientist, is the co-inventor of the **MRI (magnetic resonance imaging)** scanner. This enables doctors and researchers to obtain exact and non-invasive images of human internal organs and has revolutionised diagnostic medicine.
- The inventor of the **World Wide Web**, Sir Tim Berners-Lee (1955–), is British. Information was successfully transferred via the web for the first time on 25 December 1990.

Patient being positioned for MRI scan
Photo: Ptrump16

Problems in the economy in the 1970s

In the late 1970s, the post-war economic boom came to an end. Prices of goods and raw materials began to rise sharply and the exchange rate between the pound and other currencies was unstable. This caused problems with the 'balance of payments': imports of goods were valued at more than the price paid for exports.

Many industries and services were affected by strikes and this caused problems between the trade unions and the government. People began to argue that the unions were too powerful and that their activities were harming the UK.

The 1970s were also a time of serious unrest in Northern Ireland. In 1972, the Northern Ireland Parliament was suspended and Northern Ireland was directly ruled by the UK government. Some 3,000 people lost their lives in the decades after 1969 in the violence in Northern Ireland.

> **Mary Peters (1939–)**
> Born in Manchester, Mary Peters moved to Northern Ireland as a child. She was a talented athlete who won an Olympic gold medal in the pentathlon in 1972. After this, she raised money for local athletics and became the team manager for the women's British Olympic team. She continues to promote sport and tourism in Northern Ireland and was made a Dame of the British Empire in 2000 in recognition of her work.

Europe and the Common Market

West Germany, France, Belgium, Italy, Luxembourg and the Netherlands formed the European Economic Community (EEC) in 1957. At first the UK did not wish to join the EEC but it eventually did so in 1973. The UK remained a full member of the European Union – but did not use the Euro currency – until June 2016, by way of a referendum, the UK chose to leave the European Union.

> ### Roald Dahl (1916-1990)
> Roald Dahl was born in Wales to Norwegian parents. He served in the Royal Air Force during the Second World War. It was during the 1940s that he began to publish books and short stories. He is most well known for his children's books, although he also wrote for adults. His best-known works include Charlie and the Chocolate Factory and George's Marvellous Medicine. Several of his books have been made into films.

Conservative government from 1979 to1997

Margaret Thatcher, Britain's first woman Prime Minister, led the Conservative government from 1979 to 1990. The government made structural changes to the economy through the privatisation of nationalised industries and imposed legal controls on trade union powers.

M. Thatcher
photo: Marion S. Trikosko

Deregulation saw a great increase in the role of the City of London as an international centre for investments, insurance and other financial services. Traditional industries, such as shipbuilding and coal mining, declined. In 1982, Argentina invaded the Falkland Islands, a British overseas territory in the South Atlantic. A naval taskforce was sent from the UK and military action led to the recovery of the islands. John Major was Prime Minister after Mrs Thatcher, and helped establish the Northern Ireland peace process.

> ### Margaret Thatcher (1925–2013)
> Margaret Thatcher was the daughter of a grocer from Grantham in Lincolnshire. She trained as a chemist and lawyer. She was elected as a Conservative MP in 1959 and became a cabinet minister in 1970 as the Secretary of State for Education and Science. In 1975 she was elected as Leader of the Conservative Party and so became Leader of the Opposition.
> Following the Conservative victory in the General Election in 1979, Margaret Thatcher became the first woman Prime Minister of the UK. She was the longest-serving Prime Minister of the 20th century, remaining in Office until 1990. During her premiership, there were a number of important economic reforms within the UK. She worked closely with the United States President, Ronald Reagan, and was one of the first Western leaders to recognise and welcome the changes in the leadership of the Soviet Union which eventually led to the end of the Cold War.

Labour government from 1997-2010

In 1997 the Labour Party led by Tony Blair was elected. The Blair government introduced a Scottish Parliament and a Welsh Assembly (see Devolved Administrations). The Scottish Parliament has substantial powers to legislate. The Welsh Assembly was given fewer legislative powers but considerable control over public services. In Northern Ireland, the Blair government was able to build on the peace process, resulting in the Good Friday Agreement signed in 1998. The Northern Ireland Assembly was elected in 1999 but suspended in 2002. It was not reinstated until 2007. Most paramilitary groups in Northern Ireland have decommissioned their arms and are inactive. Gordon Brown took over as Prime Minister in 2007.

The Good Friday Agreement of 1997 brings peace in Northern Ireland.

Conflicts in Afghanistan and Iraq

Throughout the 1990s, Britain played a leading role in coalition forces involved in the liberation of Kuwait, following the Iraqi invasion in 1990, and the conflict in the Former Republic of Yugoslavia. Since 2000, British armed forces have been engaged in the global fight against international terrorism and against the proliferation of weapons of mass destruction, including operations in Afghanistan and Iraq. British combat troops left Iraq in 2009. The UK also operated in Afghanistan as part of the United Nations (UN) mandated 50-nation International Security Assistance Force. The Force has now left Afghanistan.

Coalition government from 2010-2015

In May 2010, and for the first time in the UK since February 1974, no political party won an overall majority in the General Election. The Conservative and Liberal Democrat parties formed a coalition and the leader of the Conservative Party, David Cameron, became Prime Minister.

Conservative Government from 2015 onward

In the General Elections of 2015, the Conservative party won an outright majority and David Cameron remained Prime Minister, but this time formed a fully Conservative government.

The EU referendum of 2016 and the aftermath

During the campaign of 2015, David Cameron made a pledge to renegotiate British membership of the European Union (EU). In 2016, a referendum took place, called the Brexit referendum in a contraction of the words Britain and exit. The result was 51.6% votes in favour of leaving the European Union. Having been in favour of the remaining option throughout, David Cameron resigned and was succeeded by Theresa May on July 2016. Theresa May organised a new General Election in 2017. The Conservative won, but narrowly after Theresa May secured the support of the Democratic Unionist Party (DUP) from Northern Ireland and entered negotiations to leave the EU.

2019 change of Prime Minister

The Prime minister, Theresa May, announced on May 24th 2019 that she would resign as leader of the Conservative Party on June 7th. This triggered a leadership contest within the party. The next leader would also become Prime Minister. The choice was put to the vote of all members of the Conservative Party. Boris Johnson won. On July 24th, the Queen accepted Theresa May's resignation and appointed Boris Johnson as Prime Minister.

Although he promised the UK would leave the European Union on October 31st, this was not to be the case and a further extension to January 31st, 2020 was given to the UK. British parliament and government couldn't find an agreement to resolve the Brexit issue and so a general election was called for the 12th December 2019.

General Elections of December 2019
On the 12th of December, the people of the United Kingdom was called to choose their MPs. The results were in favour of the Conservative party and Boris Johnson was confirmed as Prime Minister by the Queen. He modified the government to focus on the topmost issue of the time: to manage Brexit through.

The United Kingdom leaves the EU on 31st January 2020
On Friday the 31st of January, at 11PM, the United Kingdom officially left the European Union. A trade deal agreement was reached on the 30th December 2020.

Key points to remember:
- After the war, the UK is exhausted. A Labour government lead by Clement Atlee is elected. It creates the NHS and social security.
- Some colonies gain their independence from the British Empire.
- The UK joins international organisations such as NATO and the EU.
- Labour shortage leads to an increase of immigration.
- The 1960s see a wave of social changes and liberalisation.
- The economy falls in the late 1970s.
- Margaret Thatcher becomes Prime Minister in 1979. She increases the role of the financial sector and strongly opposes industrial actions earning her the name of the "Iron Lady".
- Labour comes back to power with Tony Blair in 1997. They increase devolution of power to other countries of the UK and obtain peace in Northern Ireland through the Good Friday Agreement of 1997.
- Labour gets mired in controversial conflicts in Afghanistan and Iraq.
- In 2010, Labour government is replaced by a coalition between Conservatives and Liberal-Democrats.
- The Conservative government of 2015 launches a referendum on EU membership. The UK left the EU on 31 January 2020..

Test your knowledge

1. **Who was Henry VII?**
   A. The leader of the House of York
   B. The leader of the House of Lancaster
   C. The leader of the House of Buckingham
   D. The leader of the House of Leeds

2. **What British discovery was influential in the development of computer science and the modern-day computer?**
   A. The Radar
   B. The Turing machine
   C. The MRI scanner
   D. The aeroplane

3. **During the Middle Ages, a Parliament was developed in Scotland, which had three Houses called Estates. These were:**
   A. The lords, the commons and the clergy
   B. The lords, the commons and the farmers
   C. The farmers, the blacksmiths and the clergy
   D. The farmers, the blacksmiths and the teachers

4. **Which of the following was one of the most famous battles of the Hundred Years War?**
   A. The Battle of Agincourt
   B. The Battle of Bannockburn
   C. The Battle of Culloden
   D. The Battle of Waterloo

5. **What is the meaning of the term 'Habeas corpus'?**
   A. You must present the person in court
   B. You must obey the law
   C. You should go to court
   D. You should not be judged

6. **Which of the following events relates to the German bombing of London and other cities at night time during the World War II?**
   A. The Bombing
   B. The German raid
   C. The Blitz
   D. The Axis

A long and illustrious history - 6. Britain since 1945

7. **Which was the first major railway built in Britain?**
   A. High Speed 1
   B. West Coast Main Line
   C. Great Western Railway
   D. East London Line

8. **Who was the leader of the English Republic?**
   A. King Richard III
   B. Oliver Cromwell
   C. Charles II
   D. Charles I

9. **When did the Vikings first visit Britain to raid coastal towns and take away goods and slaves?**
   A. AD 600
   B. AD 790
   C. AD 789
   D. AD 804

10. **Who was the first person to lead a Roman invasion in Britain in 55 BC?**
   A. Napoleon
   B. Emperor Claudius
   C. William Caxton
   D. Julius Caesar

Answers: 1.B - 2.B - 3.A - 4.A - 5.A - 6.C - 7.C - 8.B - 9.C - 10.D

A modern, thriving society

In this chapter you will learn about the population and culture of the UK. The start of the chapter shows you where the major cities of the UK are. You should be sure you can identify the various cities, such as Leeds and Bradford, confidently. Because the UK is a multicultural country you will also have to know the sizes of the different ethnic and religious groups in the UK, as well as their main festivals. The chapter focuses on British culture .

Make sure that you know and understand:
- Who each of the people described are and what they have achieved.
- Britain's sporting success and general information about sport in the UK.
- the poems, films, books and other works listed.
- the artists, composers, architects, authors, poets and other famous people.
- the extracts of poems provided.
- the famous landmarks at the end of the chapter.

1. The UK today

The UK today is a more diverse society than it was 100 years ago, in both ethnic and religious terms. Post-war immigration means that nearly 10% of the population has a parent or grandparent born outside the UK. The UK continues to be a multinational and multiracial society with a rich and varied culture. This section will tell you about the different parts of the UK and some of the important places. It will also explain some of the UK's traditions, customs and some of the popular activities that take place.

The nations of the UK

The UK is located in the north west of Europe. The longest distance on the mainland is from John O'Groats on the north coast of Scotland to Land's End in the south-west corner of England. It is about 870 miles (approximately 1,400 kilometres). Most people live in towns and cities but much of Britain is still countryside. Many people continue to visit the countryside for holidays and for leisure activities such as walking, camping and fishing.

Nations of the UK UKPhoenix79, CC0, via Wikimedia Commons

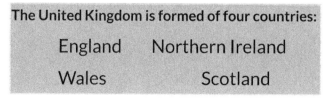

The United Kingdom is formed of four countries:

England   Northern Ireland

Wales   Scotland

Main cities of the UK

ENGLAND
- London
- Birmingham
- Liverpool
- Leeds
- Sheffield
- Bristol
- Manchester
- Bradford
- Newcastle Upon Tyne
- Plymouth
- Southampton
- Norwich

WALES
- Cardiff
- Swansea
- Newport

SCOTLAND
- Edinburgh
- Glasgow
- Dundee
- Aberdeen

NORTHERN IRELAND
- Belfast

The Capital Cities of the UK:

England	London
Northern Ireland	Belfast
Wales	Cardiff
Scotland	Edinburgh

UK currency

The currency in the UK is the pound sterling (symbol **£**). There are 100 pence in a pound.

The denominations (values) of currency are:
Coins: 1p, 2p, 5p, 10p, 20p, 50p, £1 and £2
Notes: £5, £10, £20, £50.

*£10 bank note featuring Queen Elizabeth II
Current and legal tender in 2023*

*£10 bank note featuring King Charles III
Expected to be in circulation mid-2024*

Northern Ireland and Scotland have their own banknotes, which are valid everywhere in the UK. However, shops and businesses do not have to accept them.

Languages and dialects

There are many variations in language in the different parts of the UK. The English language has many accents and dialects. In Wales, many people speak Welsh – a completely different language from English – and it is taught in schools and universities. In Scotland, Gaelic (again, a different language) is spoken in some parts of the Highlands and Islands, and in Northern Ireland some people speak Irish Gaelic.

A modern, thriving society - 1. The UK today

An ageing population

People in the UK are living longer than ever before. This is due to improved living standards and better health care. There are now a record number of people aged 85 and over. This has an impact on the cost of pensions and health care.

Population growth has been faster in more recent years. Migration into the UK and longer life expectancy have played a part in population growth. The population is very unequally distributed over the four parts of the UK. England more or less consistently makes up 84% of the total population, Wales around 5%, Scotland just over 8% and Northern Ireland less than 3%.

England makes up around 84% of the UK population.

Ethnic diversity

The UK population is ethnically diverse and changing rapidly, especially in large cities such as London. It is not always easy to get an exact picture of the ethnic origin of all the population. There are people in the UK with ethnic origins from all over the world. In surveys, the most common ethnic description chosen is white, which includes people of European, Australian, Canadian, New Zealand and American descent. Other significant groups are those of Asian, black and mixed descent.

An equal society

Within the UK, it is a legal requirement that men and women should not be discriminated against because of their gender or because they are, or are not, married. They have equal rights to work, own property, marry and divorce. If they are married, both parents are equally responsible for their children.

Women in Britain today make up about half of the workforce. On average, girls leave school with better qualifications than boys. More women than men study at university. Employment opportunities for women are much greater than they were in the past. Women work in all sectors of the economy, and there are now more women in high-level positions than ever before, including senior managers in traditionally male-dominated occupations. Alongside this, men now work in more varied jobs than they did in the past.

It is no longer expected that women should stay at home and not work. Women often continue to work after having children. In many families today, both partners work and both share responsibility for childcare and household chores.

Key points to remember:
- The United Kingdom if formed of 4 countries:
  England, Northern Ireland, Wales and Scotland.
- The currency is the pound sterling (£). 100 pence make 1 pound.
- The official language is English. Welsh is also spoken in Wales, Gaelic in Scotland and in Northern Ireland some speak Irish Gaelic.
- The population, diverse in its origin, is ageing throughout the UK.
- Men and Women have equal rights.

2. Religion

The UK is historically a Christian country. In the 2009 Citizenship Survey, 70% of people identified themselves as Christian. Much smaller proportions identified themselves as Muslim (4%), Hindu (2%), Sikh (1%), Jewish or Buddhist (both less than 0.5%), and 2% of people followed another religion. There are religious buildings for other religions all over the UK. This includes Islamic mosques, Hindu temples, Jewish synagogues, Sikh gurdwaras and Buddhist temples. However, everyone has the legal right to choose their religion, or to choose not to practise a religion. In the Citizenship Survey, 21% of people said that they had no religion. *Note: in the 2021 census, 46.2% of people identified themselves as Christians, a marked reduction from prior census.*

> The monarch is the head of the Church of England.

Christian Churches

In England, there is a constitutional link between Church and state. The official Church of the state is the Church of England (called the Anglican Church in other countries and the Episcopal Church in Scotland and the United States). It is a Protestant Church and has existed since the Reformation in the 1530s (see Religious Conflicts section).

Canterbury Cathedral - photo: Antony McCallum

The monarch is the head of the Church of England. The spiritual leader of the Church of England is the Archbishop of Canterbury. The monarch has the right to select the Archbishop and other senior church officials, but usually the choice is made by the Prime Minister and a committee appointed by the Church. Several Church of England bishops sit in the House of Lords (see House of Lords).

In Scotland, the national Church is the Church of Scotland, which is a Presbyterian Church. It is governed by ministers and elders. The chairperson of the General Assembly of the Church of Scotland is the Moderator, who is appointed for one year only and often speaks on behalf of that Church.

There is no established Church in Wales or Northern Ireland. Other Protestant Christian groups in the UK are Baptists, Methodists, Presbyterians and Quakers. There are also other denominations of Christianity, the biggest of which is Roman Catholic.

Patron Saints' days

England, Scotland, Wales and Northern Ireland have a national saint, called a patron saint.

Each country of the UK has a Saint and a Special day		
England	23 April	St George
Northern Ireland	17 March	St Patrick
Wales	1 March	St David
Scotland	30 November	St Andrew

Only Scotland and Northern Ireland have their patron saint's day as an official holiday (although in Scotland not all businesses and Offices will close). Events are held across Scotland, Northern Ireland and the rest of the country, especially where there are a lot of people of Scottish, Northern Irish and Irish heritage.

While the patron saints' days are no longer public holidays in England and Wales, they are still celebrated. Parades and small festivals are held all over the two countries.

Key points to remember:
- The main religion in the UK is Christian.
- In England, the official Church is the Church of England, headed by the monarch.
- The spiritual leader of the Church of England is the Archbishop of Canterbury.
- In Scotland, the Church of Scotland is governed by ministers and elders.
- Each country celebrates its own patron saint.

3. Customs and traditions

The main Christian festivals

Christmas Tree, Trafalgar Square - photo: Robin Sones

Christmas Day, 25 December, celebrates the birth of Jesus Christ. It is a public holiday. Many Christians go to church on Christmas Eve (24 December) or on Christmas Day itself. Christmas is celebrated in a traditional way. People usually spend the day at home and eat a special meal, which often includes roast turkey, Christmas pudding and mince pies. They give gifts, send cards and decorate their houses. Christmas is a special time for children. Very young children believe that Father Christmas (also known as Santa Claus) brings them presents during the night before Christmas Day. Many people decorate a tree in their home. Boxing Day is the day after Christmas Day and is a public holiday.

Easter takes place in March or April. It marks the death of Jesus Christ on Good Friday and his rising from the dead on Easter Sunday. Both Good Friday and the following Monday, called Easter Monday, are public holidays.

The 40 days before Easter are known as Lent. It is a time when Christians take time to reflect and prepare for Easter. Traditionally, people would fast during this period and today many people will give something up, like a favourite food. The day before Lent starts is called Shrove Tuesday, or Pancake Day. People eat pancakes, which were traditionally made to use up foods such as eggs, fat and milk before fasting. Lent begins on Ash Wednesday. There are church services where Christians are marked with an ash cross on their forehead as a symbol of death and sorrow for sin. Easter is also celebrated by people who are not religious. 'Easter eggs' are chocolate eggs often given as presents at Easter as a symbol of new life.

Shrove Tuesday	Day before Lent
Ash Wednesday	Start of Lent
Lent	40 days before Easter
Easter Sunday	Sunday following first full moon after 20 March
Christmas Eve	24 December
Christmas Day	25 December
Boxing Day	26 December

Other religious festivals

- **Diwali** normally falls in October or November and lasts for five days. It is often called the Festival of Lights. It is celebrated by Hindus and Sikhs. It celebrates the victory of good over evil and the gaining of knowledge. There are different stories about how the festival came about. There is a famous celebration of Diwali in Leicester.
- **Hannukah** is in November or December and is celebrated for eight days. It is to remember the Jews' struggle for religious freedom. On each day of the festival a candle is lit on a stand of eight candles (called a menorah) to remember the story of the festival, where oil that should have lasted only a day did so for eight.
- **Eid al-Fitr** celebrates the end of Ramadan, when Muslims have fasted for a month. They thank Allah for giving them the strength to complete the fast. The date when it takes place changes every year. Muslims attend special services and meals.
- **Eid ul Adha** remembers that the prophet Ibrahim was willing to sacrifice his son when God ordered him to. It reminds Muslims of their own commitment to God. Many Muslims sacrifice an animal to eat during this festival. In Britain this has to be done in a slaughterhouse.
- **Vaisakhi** (also spelled Baisakhi) is a Sikh festival which celebrates the founding of the Sikh community known as the Khalsa. It is celebrated on 14 April each year with parades, dancing and singing.

Diwali	Hindus and Sikhs	5 days in October or November
Hanukah	Jews	8 days in November or December
Eid al-Fitr	Muslims	end of Ramadan
Eid ul Adha	Muslims	10th day of last month in Islamic year
Vaisakhi	Sikhs	14 April

Other festivals and traditions

- **New Year**, 1 January, is a public holiday. People usually celebrate on the night of 31 December (called New Year's Eve). In Scotland, 31 December is called Hogmanay and 2 January is also a public holiday. For some Scottish people, Hogmanay is a bigger holiday than Christmas.
- **Valentine's Day**, 14 February, is when lovers exchange cards and gifts. Sometimes people send anonymous cards to someone they secretly admire.
- **April Fool's Day**, 1 April, is a day when people play jokes on each other until midday. The television and newspapers often have stories that are April Fool jokes.
- **Mothering Sunday (or Mother's Day)** is the Sunday three weeks before Easter. Children send cards or buy gifts for their mothers.

A modern, thriving society - 3. Customs and traditions

- **Father's Day** is the third Sunday in June. Children buy cards or gifts for their fathers.
- **Halloween**, 31 October, is an ancient festival and has roots in the pagan festival to mark the beginning of winter. Young people will often dress up in frightening costumes to play 'trick or treat'. People give them treats to stop them playing tricks on them. A lot of people carve lanterns out of pumpkins and put a candle inside.
- **Bonfire Night**, 5 November, is an occasion when people in Great Britain set off fireworks at home or in special displays. The origin of this celebration was an event in 1605, when a group of Catholics led by Guy Fawkes failed in their plan to kill the Protestant king with a bomb in the Houses of Parliament.
- **Remembrance Day**, 11 November, commemorates those who died fighting for the UK and its allies. Originally it commemorated the dead of the First World War, which ended on 11 November 1918. People wear poppies (the red flower found on the battlefields of the First World War). At 11.00 am there is a two-minute silence and wreaths are laid at the Cenotaph in Whitehall, London.

Bank holidays

As well as those mentioned previously, there are other public holidays each year called bank holidays, when banks and many other businesses are closed for the day. These are of no religious significance. They are at the beginning of May, in late May or early June, and in August. In Northern Ireland, the anniversary of the Battle of the Boyne in July is also a public holiday.

January, 1	New Year
February, 14	Valentine's Day
April, 1	April Fool's Day
Sunday, 3 weeks before Easter	Mother's Day
1st Monday of May	Bank Holiday
Last Monday of May	Bank Holiday
3rd Sunday in June	Father's Day
Last Monday of August	Bank Holiday
October, 31	Halloween
November, 5	Bonfire Night
November, 11	Remembrance Day
December, 24	Christmas Eve
December, 25	Christmas Day
December, 26	Boxing Day

Key points to remember:
- The UK celebrates Christian festivals such as Easter, Lent and the birth of Jesus.
- Other religious festivals are celebrated from Muslims, Hindus and Sick traditions.
- Bank holidays are public holidays, usually on a Monday.
- The UK celebrates historical events such as Remembrance Day or Bonfire Night.
- There are also special days for lovers or parents.
- Christmas is an important celebration across the country.

4. Sport

Sports of all kinds play an important part in many people's lives. There are several sports that are particularly popular in the UK. Many sporting events take place at major stadiums such as Wembley Stadium in London and the Millennium Stadium in Cardiff.

Local governments and private companies provide sports facilities such as swimming pools, tennis courts, football pitches, dry ski slopes and gymnasiums. Many famous sports, including cricket, football, lawn tennis, golf and rugby, began in Britain.

The UK has hosted the Olympic Games on three occasions: 1908, 1948 and 2012. The main Olympic site for the 2012 Games was in Stratford, East London. The British team was very successful, across a wide range of Olympic sports, finishing third in the medal table.

Horse Parade Grounds, The Mall, London 2012 Olympics - Photo: Ank kumar

The Paralympic Games for 2012 were also hosted in London. The Paralympics have their origin in the work of Dr Sir Ludwig Guttman, a German refugee, at the Stoke Mandeville hospital in Buckinghamshire. Dr Guttman developed new methods of treatment for people with spinal injuries and encouraged patients to take part in exercise and sport.

Notable British sportsmen and women
- **Sir Roger Bannister** (1929–2018) was the first man in the world to run a mile in under four minutes, in 1954.
- **Sir Jackie Stewart** (1939–) is a Scottish former racing driver who won the Formula 1 world championship three times.
- **Bobby Moore** (1941–93) captained the English football team that won the World Cup in 1966.
- **Sir Ian Botham** (1955–) captained the English cricket team and holds a number of English Test cricket records, both for batting and for bowling.
- **Jayne Torvill** (1957–) and Christopher Dean (1958–) won gold medals for ice dancing at the Olympic Games in 1984 and in four consecutive world championships.
- **Sir Steve Redgrave** (1962–) won gold medals in rowing in five consecutive Olympic Games and is one of Britain's greatest Olympians.
- **Baroness Tanni-Grey Thompson** (1969–) is an athlete who uses a wheelchair and won 16 Paralympic medals, including 11 gold medals, in races over five Paralympic Games. She won the London Marathon six times and broke a total of 30 world records.
- **Dame Kelly Holmes** (1970–) won two gold medals for running in the 2004 Olympic Games. She has held a number of British and European records.
- **Dame Ellen MacArthur** (1976–) is a yachtswoman and in 2004 became the fastest person to sail around the world singlehanded.

- **Sir Chris Hoy** (1976–) is a Scottish cyclist who has won six gold and one silver Olympic medals. He has also won 11 world championship titles.
- **David Weir** (1979–) is a Paralympian who uses a wheelchair and has won six gold medals over two Paralympic Games. He has also won the London Marathon six times.
- **Bradley Wiggins** (1980–) is a cyclist. In 2012, he became the first Briton to win the Tour de France. He has won seven Olympic medals, including gold medals in the 2004, 2008 and 2012 Olympic Games.
- **Mo Farah** (1983–) is a British distance runner, born in Somalia. He won gold medals in the 2012 Olympics for the 5,000 and 10,000 metres and is the first Briton to win the Olympic gold medal in the 10,000 metres.
- **Jessica Ennis** (1986–) is an athlete. She won the 2012 Olympic gold medal in the heptathlon, which includes seven different track and field events. She also holds a number of British athletics records.
- **Andy Murray** (1987–) is a Scottish tennis player who in 2012 won the men's singles in the US Open. He is the first British man to win a singles title in a Grand Slam tournament since 1936. In the same year, he won Olympic gold and silver medals and was runner-up in the men's singles at Wimbledon (see Tennis).
- **Ellie Simmonds** (1994–) is a Paralympian who won gold medals for swimming at the 2008 and 2012 Paralympic Games and holds a number of world records. She was the youngest member of the British team at the 2008 Games.

Cricket

Cricket originated in England and is now played in many countries. Games can last up to five days but still result in a draw! The idiosyncratic nature of the game and its complex laws are said to reflect the best of the British character and sense of fair play. You may come across expressions such as 'rain stopped play', 'batting on a sticky wicket', 'playing a straight bat', 'bowled a googly' or 'it's just not cricket', which have passed into everyday usage. The most famous competition is the Ashes, which is a series of Test matches played between England and Australia.

County cricket at The Oval, London
Photo: John Sutton

Football

Football is the UK's most popular sport. It has a long history in the UK and the first professional football clubs were formed in the late 19th century.

Sunday football on Millwall Park, London
Photo: Peter Thwaite

England, Scotland, Wales and Northern Ireland each have separate leagues in which clubs representing different towns and cities compete. The English Premier League attracts a huge international audience. Many of the best players in the world play in the Premier League. Many UK teams also compete in competitions such as the UEFA (Union of European Football Associations) Champions League, against other teams from Europe. Most towns and cities have a professional club and people take great pride in supporting their home team. There can be great rivalry between different football clubs and among fans.

Each country in the UK also has its own national team that competes with other national teams across the world in tournaments such as the FIFA (Fédération Internationale de Football Association) World Cup and the UEFA European Football Championships. For the men, England's last international tournament victory was for at the World Cup of 1966, hosted in the UK. But in 2022, the women team nicknamed the Lionesses, became European Champions after beating Germany at Wembley stadium. Football is also a popular sport to play in many local communities, with people playing amateur games every week in parks all over the UK.

England Women v Scotland Women (RBS 6 Nations) - Photo: Steve

Rugby

Rugby originated in England in the early 19th century and is very popular in the UK today. There are two different types of rugby, which have different rules: union and league. Both have separate leagues and national teams in England, Wales, Scotland and Northern Ireland (who play with the Irish Republic). Teams from all countries compete in a range of competitions. The most famous rugby union competition is the Six Nations Championship between England, Ireland, Scotland, Wales, France and Italy. The Super League is the most well-known rugby league (club) competition.

Horse-racing

There is a very long history of horse racing in Britain, with evidence of events taking place as far back as Roman times. The sport has a long association with royalty. There are racecourses all over the UK. Famous horse-racing events include: Royal Ascot, a five-day race meeting in Berkshire attended by members of the Royal Family; the

Frankel the horse winning at Doncaster (2010) photo: RacingKel

Grand National at Aintree near Liverpool; and the Scottish Grand National at Ayr. There is a National Horseracing Museum in Newmarket, Suffolk.

Golf

The modern game of golf can be traced back to 15th century Scotland. It is a popular sport played socially as well as professionally. There are public and private golf courses all over the UK. St Andrews in Scotland is known as the home of golf. The Open Championship is the only 'Major' tournament held outside the United States. It is hosted by a different golf course every year.

Laura Robson at Wimbledon (2008)
Photo: Riversoflife.

Tennis

Modern tennis evolved in England in the late 19th century. The first tennis club was founded in Leamington Spa in 1872. The most famous tournament hosted in Britain is The Wimbledon Championships, which takes place each year at the All England Lawn Tennis and Croquet Club. It is the oldest tennis tournament in the world and the only 'Grand Slam' event played on grass.

Water sports

Sailing continues to be popular in the UK, reflecting our maritime heritage. A British sailor, Sir Francis Chichester, was the first person to sail single-handed around the world, in 1966/67. Two years later, Sir Robin Knox-Johnston became the first person to do this without stopping. Many sailing events are held throughout the UK, the most famous of which is at Cowes on the Isle of Wight. Rowing is also popular, both as a leisure activity and as a competitive sport. There is a popular yearly race on the Thames between Oxford and Cambridge Universities.

Oxford v Cambridge Boat Race 2012
in Hammersmith - Photo: ale

Motor sports

There is a long history of motor sport in the UK, for both cars and motor cycles. Motor-car racing in the UK started in 1902. The UK continues to be a world leader in the development and manufacture of motor-sport technology. A Formula 1 Grand Prix event is held in the UK each year and a number of British Grand Prix drivers have won the Formula 1 World Championship. Recent British winners include Damon Hill, Lewis Hamilton and Jensen Button.

Skiing

Skiing is increasingly popular in the UK. Many people go abroad to ski and there are also dry ski slopes throughout the UK. Skiing on snow may also be possible during the winter. There are five ski centres in Scotland, as well as Europe's longest dry ski slope near Edinburgh.

Key points to remember:

- The UK has a long tradition of playing sports and even invented or helped popularise several.
- In 2012, the UK hosted the Olympic and Paralympic Games.
- Important British sports include Cricket, Rugby, Football and Tennis.
- Horse-racing is very close to the Royal Family and can be large social events for the high society (for instance the Grand National).
- There are dry ski slopes in the UK, many of which are in Scotland.
- In 2022, The Lionesses became football European Champions.

5. Arts and culture

Music

Music is an important part of British culture, with a rich and varied heritage. It ranges from classical music to modern pop. There are many different venues and musical events that take place across the UK.

BBC Proms- photo: Yuichi

The Proms is an eight-week summer season of orchestral classical music that takes place in various venues, including the Royal Albert Hall in London. It has been organised by the British Broadcasting Corporation (BBC) since 1927. The Last Night of the Proms is the most well-known concert and (along with others in the series) is broadcast on television.

Classical music has been popular in the UK for many centuries. **Henry Purcell** (1659–95) was the organist at Westminster Abbey. He wrote church music, operas and other pieces, and developed a British style distinct from that elsewhere in Europe. He continues to be influential on British composers.

The German-born composer **George Frederick Handel** (1695–1759) spent many years in the UK and became a British citizen in 1727. He wrote the Water Music for King George I and Music for the Royal Fireworks for his son, George II. Both these pieces continue to be very popular. Handel also wrote an oratorio, Messiah, which is sung regularly by choirs, often at Easter time.

More recently, important composers include **Gustav Holst** (1874–1934), whose work includes The Planets, a suite of pieces themed around the planets of the solar system. He adapted Jupiter, part of the Planets suite, as the tune for I vow to thee my country, a popular hymn in British churches.

- **Sir Edward Elgar** (1857–1934) was born in Worcester, England. His best-known work is probably the Pomp and Circumstance Marches. March No 1 (Land of Hope and Glory) is usually played at the Last Night of the Proms at the Royal Albert Hall.
- **Ralph Vaughan Williams** (1872–1958) wrote music for orchestras and choirs. He was strongly influenced by traditional English folk music.
- **Sir William Walton** (1902–83) wrote a wide range of music, from film scores to opera. He wrote marches for the coronations of King George VI and Queen Elizabeth II but his best-known works are probably Façade, which became a ballet, and Balthazar's Feast, which is intended to be sung by a large choir.
- **Benjamin Britten** (1913–76) is best known for his operas, which include Peter

Grimes and Billy Budd. He also wrote A Young Person's Guide to the Orchestra, which is based on a piece of music by Purcell and introduces the listener to the various different sections of an orchestra. He founded the Aldeburgh festival in Suffolk, which continues to be a popular music event of international importance.

Other types of popular music, including folk, jazz, and pop music, have flourished in Britain since the 20th century. Britain has had an impact on popular music around the world, due to the wide use of the English language, the UK's cultural links with many countries, and British capacity for invention and innovation. Since the 1960s, British pop music has made one of the most important cultural contributions to life in the UK. Bands including The Beatles and The Rolling Stones continue to have an influence

on music both here and abroad. British pop music has continued to innovate – for example, the Punk movement of the late 1970s, and the trend towards boy and girl bands in the 1990s.

Beatles ad 1965 'just the beatles'

The Spice Girls - Italia 1997

There are many large venues that host music events throughout the year, such as: Wembley Stadium; The O2 in Greenwich, south-east London; and the Scottish Exhibition and Conference Centre (SECC) in Glasgow.

Festival season takes place across the UK every summer, with major events in various locations. Famous festivals include Glastonbury, the Isle of Wight Festival and the V Festival. Many bands and solo artists, both well-known and up-and-coming, perform at these events.

The National Eisteddfod of Wales is an annual cultural festival which includes music, dance, art and original performances largely in Welsh. It

Isle of Wight Festival 2014 main stage
Photo: Liz Murray Photography

includes a number of important competitions for Welsh poetry.

The Mercury Music Prize is awarded each September for the best album from the UK and Ireland. The Brit Awards is an annual event that gives awards in a range of categories, such as best British group and best British solo artist.

Theatre
There are theatres in most towns and cities throughout the UK, ranging from the large to the small. They are an important part of local communities and often show both professional and amateur productions. London's West End, also known as 'Theatreland', is particularly

well known. The Mousetrap, a murder-mystery play by Dame Agatha Christie, has been running in the West End since 1952 and has had the longest initial run of any show in history.

There is also a strong tradition of musical theatre in the UK. In the 19th century, Gilbert and Sullivan wrote comic operas, often making fun of popular culture and politics. These operas include HMS Pinafore, The Pirates of Penzance and The Mikado. Gilbert and Sullivan's work is still often staged by professional and amateur groups. More recently, Andrew Lloyd Webber has written the music for shows which have been popular throughout the world, including, in collaboration with Tim Rice, Jesus Christ Superstar and Evita, and also Cats and The Phantom of the Opera.

One British tradition is the pantomime. Many theatres produce a pantomime at Christmas time. They are based on fairy stories and are light-hearted plays with music and comedy, enjoyed by family audiences. One of the traditional characters is the Dame, a woman played by a man. There is often also a pantomime horse or cow played by two actors in the same costume.

Pantomime dames - Photo: Roogi

The Edinburgh Festival takes place in Edinburgh, Scotland, every summer. It is a series of different arts and cultural festivals, with the biggest and most well-known being the Edinburgh Festival Fringe ('the Fringe'). The Fringe is a showcase of mainly theatre and comedy performances. It often shows experimental work.

The Laurence Olivier Awards take place annually at different venues in London. There are a variety of categories, including best director, best actor and best actress. The awards are named after the British actor Sir Laurence Olivier, later Lord Olivier, who was best known for his roles in various Shakespeare plays.

Art

During the Middle Ages, most art had a religious theme, particularly wall paintings in churches and illustrations in religious books. Much of this was lost after the Protestant Reformation but wealthy families began to collect other paintings and sculptures. Many of the painters working in Britain in the 16th and 17th centuries were from abroad – for example, Hans Holbein and Sir Anthony Van Dyck. British artists, particularly those painting portraits and landscapes, became well known from the 18th century onwards.

National Museum Cardiff
Photo: Ham II

Works by British and international artists are displayed in galleries across the UK. Some of the most well-known galleries are The National Gallery, Tate Britain and Tate Modern in London, the National Museum in Cardiff, and the National Gallery of Scotland in Edinburgh.

A modern, thriving society - 5. Arts and culture

The Turner Prize was established in 1984 and celebrates contemporary art. It was named after Joseph Turner. Four works are shortlisted every year and shown at Tate Britain before the winner is announced. The Turner Prize is recognised as one of the most prestigious visual art awards in Europe. Previous winners include Damien Hirst and Richard Wright.

Tate Modern, London
Photo: Robin Webster

Notable British artists

- **Thomas Gainsborough** (1727–88) was a portrait painter who often painted people in country or garden scenery.
- **David Allan** (1744–96) was a Scottish painter who was best known for painting portraits. One of his most famous works is called The Origin of Painting.
- **Joseph Turner** (1775–1851) was an influential landscape painter in a modern style. He is considered the artist who raised the profile of landscape painting.
- **John Constable** (1776–1837) was a landscape painter most famous for his works of Dedham Vale on the Suffolk–Essex border in the east of England.
- The Pre-Raphaelites were an important group of artists in the second half of the 19th century. They painted detailed pictures on religious or literary themes in bright colours. They included **Holman Hunt**, **Dante Gabriel Rossetti** and **Sir John Millais**.
- **Sir John Lavery** (1856–1941) was a very successful Northern Irish portrait painter. His work included painting the Royal Family.
- **Henry Moore** (1898–1986) was an English sculptor and artist. He is best known for his large bronze abstract sculptures.
- **John Petts** (1914–91) was a Welsh artist, best known for his engravings and stained glass.
- **Lucian Freud** (1922–2011) was a German-born British artist. He is best known for his portraits.
- **David Hockney** (1937–) was an important contributor to the 'pop art' movement of the 1960s and continues to be influential today.

Architecture

The architectural heritage of the UK is rich and varied. In the Middle Ages, great cathedrals and churches were built, many of which still stand today. Examples are the cathedrals in Durham, Lincoln, Canterbury and Salisbury. The White Tower in the Tower of London is an example of a Norman castle keep, built on the orders of William the Conqueror (see The Norman Conquest and The Tower of London).

Gradually, as the countryside became more peaceful and landowners became richer, the houses of the wealthy became more elaborate and great country houses such as Hardwick Hall in Derbyshire were built. British styles of architecture began to evolve.

In the 17th century, Inigo Jones took inspiration from classical architecture to design the Queen's House at Greenwich and the Banqueting House in Whitehall in London. Later in the century, Sir Christopher Wren helped develop a British version of the ornate styles popular in Europe in buildings such as the new St Paul's Cathedral.

In the 18th century, simpler designs became popular. The Scottish architect Robert Adam influenced the development of architecture in the UK, Europe and America. He designed the inside decoration as well as the building itself in great houses such as Dumfries House in Scotland. His ideas influenced architects in cities such as Bath, where the Royal Crescent was built.

Dumfries House front
Photo: Julien.scavini

Royal Crescent Bath - Photo: Neil Parley

In the 19th century, the medieval 'gothic' style became popular again. As cities expanded, many great public buildings were built in this style. The Houses of Parliament and St Pancras Station were built at this time, as were the town halls in cities such as Manchester and Sheffield.

In the 20th century, Sir Edwin Lutyens had an influence throughout the British Empire. He designed New Delhi to be the seat of government in India. After the First World War, he was responsible for many war memorials throughout the world, including the Cenotaph in Whitehall. The Cenotaph is the site of the annual Remembrance Day service attended by the Queen, politicians and foreign ambassadors.

The Cenotaph, Whitehall, London
Photo: Paul the Archivist

Modern British architects including Sir Norman Foster, Lord (Richard) Rogers and Dame Zaha Hadid have worked on major projects throughout the world as well as within the UK.

Alongside the development of architecture, garden design and landscaping have played an important role in the UK. In the 18th century, Lancelot 'Capability' Brown designed the grounds around country houses so that the landscape appeared to be natural, with grass, trees and lakes. He often said that a place had 'capabilities'.

Later, Gertrude Jekyll often worked with Edwin Lutyens to design colourful gardens around the houses he designed. Gardens continue to be an important part of homes in the UK. The annual Chelsea Flower Show showcases garden design from Britain and around the world.

A modern, thriving society - 5. Arts and culture

Fashion and design

Britain has produced many great designers, from Thomas Chippendale (who designed furniture in the 18th century) to Clarice Cliff (who designed Art Deco ceramics) to Sir Terence Conran (a 20th-century interior designer). Leading fashion designers of recent years include Mary Quant, Alexander McQueen and Vivienne Westwood.

Literature

The UK has a prestigious literary history and tradition. Several British writers, including the novelist Sir William Golding, the poet Seamus Heaney, and the playwright Harold Pinter, have won the Nobel Prize in Literature. Other authors have become well known in popular fiction. Agatha Christie's detective stories are read all over the world and Ian Fleming's books introduced James Bond. In 2003, The Lord of the Rings by JRR Tolkien was voted the country's best-loved novel.

The Man Booker Prize for Fiction is awarded annually for the best fiction novel written by an author from the Commonwealth, Ireland or Zimbabwe. It has been awarded since 1968. Past winners include Ian McEwan, Hilary Mantel and Julian Barnes.

Notable authors and writers

- **Jane Austen** (1775–1817) was an English novelist. Her books include Pride and Prejudice and Sense and Sensibility. Her novels are concerned with marriage and family relationships. Many have been made into television programmes or films.
- **Charles Dickens** (1812–70) wrote a number of very famous novels, including Oliver Twist and Great Expectations. You will hear references in everyday talk to some of the characters in his books, such as Scrooge (a mean person) or Mr Micawber (always hopeful).
- **Robert Louis Stevenson** (1850–94) wrote books which are still read by adults and children today. His most famous books include Treasure Island, Kidnapped and Dr Jekyll and Mr Hyde.
- **Thomas Hardy** (1840–1928) was an author and poet. His best-known novels focus on rural society and include Far from the Madding Crowd and Jude the Obscure.
- **Sir Arthur Conan Doyle** (1859–1930) was a Scottish doctor and writer. He was best known for his stories about Sherlock Holmes, who was one of the first fictional detectives.
- **Evelyn Waugh** (1903–66) wrote satirical novels, including Decline and Fall and Scoop. He is perhaps best known for Brideshead Revisited.
- **Sir Kingsley Amis** (1922–95) was an English novelist and poet. He wrote more than 20 novels. The most well-known is Lucky Jim.
- **Graham Green**e (1904–91) wrote novels often influenced by his religious beliefs, including The Heart of the Matter, The Honorary Consul, Brighton Rock and Our Man in Havana.
- **J K Rowling** (1965–) wrote the Harry Potter series of children's books, which have enjoyed huge international success. She now writes fiction for adults as well.

British poets

British poetry is among the richest in the world. The Anglo-Saxon poem Beowulf tells of its hero's battles against monsters and is still translated into modern English. Poems which survive from the Middle Ages include Chaucer's Canterbury Tales and a poem called Sir Gawain and the Green Knight, about one of the knights at the court of King Arthur.

As well as plays, Shakespeare wrote many sonnets (poems which must be 14 lines long) and some longer poems. As Protestant ideas spread, a number of poets wrote poems inspired by their religious views. One of these was John Milton, who wrote Paradise Lost.

Other poets, including William Wordsworth, were inspired by nature. Sir Walter Scott wrote poems inspired by Scotland and the traditional stories and songs from the area on the borders of Scotland and England. He also wrote novels, many of which were set in Scotland.

Monument to Sir Walter Scott
Photo: Ad Meskens

Poetry was very popular in the 19th century, with poets such as William Blake, John Keats, Lord Byron, Percy Shelley, Alfred Lord Tennyson, and Robert and Elizabeth Browning. Later, many poets – for example, Wilfred Owen and Siegfried Sassoon – were inspired to write about their experiences in the First World War. More recently, popular poets have included Sir Walter de la Mare, John Masefield, Sir John Betjeman and Ted Hughes. Some of the best-known poets are buried or commemorated in Poet's Corner in Westminster Abbey.

Some famous lines include:

'Oh to be in England now that April's there
And whoever wakes in England sees, some morning, unaware,
That the lowest boughs and the brushwood sheaf
Round the elm-tree bole are in tiny leaf
While the Chaffinch sings on the orchard bough
In England – Now!'
(Robert Browning, 1812–89 – Home Thoughts from Abroad)

'I wander'd lonely as a cloud
That floats on high o'er vales and hills
When all at once I saw a crowd,
A host of golden daffodils'
(William Wordsworth, 1770–1850 – The Daffodils)

'Tyger! Tyger! Burning bright
In the forests of the night,
What immortal hand or eye
Could frame thy fearful symmetry?'
(William Blake, 1757–1827 – The Tyger)

'What passing-bells for these who die as cattle?
Only the monstrous anger of the guns.
Only the stuttering rifles' rapid rattle
Can patter out their hasty orisons.'
(Wilfred Owen, 1893–1918 – Anthem for Doomed Youth)

'She walks in beauty, like the night
Of cloudless climes and starry skies,
All that's best of dark and bright
Meet in her aspect and her eyes'
(Lord Byron, 1788–1824 – She Walks in Beauty)

Key points to remember:

- British culture is rich and diverse and goes back centuries.
- Classical music is celebrated every year in a summer festival called the Proms.
- Britain had a huge impact on pop music, notably in the 1960s and 1970s with the Beatles, the Rolling Stones and later, boys bands or girls bands (e.g. Spice Girls).
- Britain hosts music festivals like Glastonbury, the Isle of Wight and the V Festival.
- The Mousetrap by Agatha Christie is the longest running theatre play of all time.
- Pantomime is a British tradition, notably around Christmas.
- Art was mostly religious during the Middle Ages.
- Well-known British art galleries include: The National Gallery, the Tate Britain and then Tate Modern in London; The National Museum in Cardiff and the National Gallery of Scotland in Edinburgh.
- Sir Christopher Wren designed many churches in London and St Paul's Cathedral.
- Some fashion designers: Mary Quant, Vivienne Westwood, Anthony McQueen.
- The UK has a long history of literature and poetry.
- Shakespeare wrote numerous plays and poems.
- Poets were often inspired by nature like William Wordsworth.
- The Man Booker Prize is awarded for best fiction novel from the Commonwealth.

6. Leisure

People in the UK spend their leisure time in many different ways.

Gardening

A lot of people have gardens at home and will spend their free time looking after them. Some people rent additional land called 'an allotment', where they grow fruit and vegetables. Gardening and flower shows range from major national exhibitions to small local events. Many towns have garden centres selling plants and gardening equipment. There are famous gardens to visit throughout the UK, including Kew Gardens, Sissinghurst and Hidcote in England, Crathes Castle and Inveraray Castle in Scotland, Bodnant Garden in Wales, and Mount Stewart in Northern Ireland.

The countries that make up the UK all have flowers which are particularly associated with them and which are sometimes worn on national saints' days.

England - Rose   N.Ireland - Shamrock   Wales - Daffodil   Scotland - Thistle

Shopping

There are many different places to go shopping in the UK. Most towns and cities have a central shopping area, which is called the town centre. Undercover shopping centres are also common – these might be in town centres or on the outskirts of a town or city. Most shops in the UK are open seven days a week, although trading hours on Sundays and public holidays are generally reduced. Many towns also have markets on one or more days a week, where stallholders sell a variety of goods.

Shops in the UK are often open at weekends.

Cooking and food

Many people in the UK enjoy cooking. They often invite each other to their homes for dinner. A wide variety of food is eaten in the UK because of the country's rich cultural heritage and diverse population.

Traditional foods

There are a variety of foods traditionally associated with different parts of the UK:

- **England**: Roast beef, which is served with potatoes, vegetables, Yorkshire puddings (batter that is baked in the oven) and other accompaniments. Fish and chips are also popular.
- **Wales**: Welsh cakes – a traditional Welsh snack made from flour, dried fruits and spices, and served either hot or cold.
- **Scotland**: Haggis – a sheep's stomach stuffed with offal, suet, onions and oatmeal.
- **Northern Ireland**: Ulster fry – a fried meal with bacon, eggs, sausage, black pudding, white pudding, tomatoes, mushrooms, soda bread and potato bread.

Films - British film industry

Films were first shown publicly in the UK in 1896 and film screenings very quickly became popular. From the beginning, film makers became famous for clever special effects and this continues to be an area of British expertise. From the early days of the cinema, British actors have worked in both the UK and USA. Sir Charles (Charlie) Chaplin became famous in silent movies for his tramp character and was one of many British actors to make a career in Hollywood.

Charlie Chaplin from the 1940 film The Great Dictator - Trailer screenshot

British studios flourished in the 1930s. Eminent directors included Sir Alexander Korda and Sir Alfred Hitchcock, who later left for Hollywood and remained an important film director until his death in 1980. During the Second World War, British movies (for example, In Which We Serve) played an important part in boosting morale. Later, British directors including Sir David Lean and Ridley Scott found great success both in the UK and internationally.

The 1950s and 1960s were a high point for British comedies, including Passport to

Pimlico, The Ladykillers and, later, the Carry On films. Many of the films now produced in the UK are made by foreign companies, using British expertise. Some of the most commercially successful films of all time, including the two highest-grossing film franchises (Harry Potter and James Bond), have been produced in the UK. Ealing Studios has a claim to being the oldest continuously working film studio facility in the world. Britain continues to be particularly strong in special effects and animation. One example is the work of Nick Park, who has won four

Ealing Studios London
Photo: Rod Allday

Oscars for his animated films, including three for films featuring Wallace and Gromit.

Actors such as Sir Lawrence Olivier, David Niven, Sir Rex Harrison and Richard Burton starred in a wide variety of popular films. British actors continue to be popular and continue to win awards throughout the world. Recent British actors to have won Oscars include Colin Firth, Sir Antony Hopkins, Dame Judi Dench, Kate Winslet and Tilda Swinton. The annual British Academy Film Awards, hosted by the British Academy of Film and Television Arts (BAFTA), are the British equivalent of the Oscars.

British Oscar winners include: Colin Firth, Kate Winslet, Tilda Swinton, Dame Judi Dench, Sir Anthony Hopkins.

Some famous British films

- **The 39 Steps** (1935), directed by Alfred Hitchcock
- **Brief Encounter** (1945), directed by David Lean
- **The Third Man** (1949), directed by Carol Reed
- **The Belles of St Trinian's** (1954), directed by Frank Launder
- **Lawrence of Arabia** (1962), directed by David Lean
- **Women in Love** (1969), directed by Ken Russell
- **Don't Look Now** (1973), directed by Nicolas Roeg
- **Chariots of Fire** (1981), directed by Hugh Hudson
- **The Killing Fields** (1984), directed by Roland Joffé
- **Four Weddings and a Funeral** (1994), directed by Mike Newell
- **Touching the Void** (2003), directed by Kevin MacDonald.

British comedy

The traditions of comedy and satire, and the ability to laugh at ourselves, are an important part of the UK character. Medieval kings and rich nobles had jesters who told jokes and made fun of people in the Court. Later, Shakespeare included comic characters in his plays. In the 18th century, political cartoons attacking prominent politicians – and, sometimes, the monarch or other members of the Royal Family – became increasingly popular. In the 19th century, satirical magazines began to be published. The most famous was Punch, which was published for the first time in the 1840s. Today, political cartoons continue to be published in newspapers, and magazines such as Private Eye continue the tradition of satire.

Comedians were a popular feature of British music hall, a form of variety theatre which was very common until television became the leading form of entertainment in the UK. Some of the people who had performed in the music halls in the 1940s and 1950s, such as Morecambe and Wise, became stars of television.

Television comedy developed its own style. Situation comedies, or sitcoms, which often look at family life and relationships in the workplace, remain popular. Satire has also continued to be important, with shows like That Was The Week That Was in the 1960s and Spitting Image in the 1980s and 1990s. In 1969, Monty Python's Flying Circus introduced a new type of progressive comedy. Stand-up comedy, where a solo comedian talks to a live audience, has become popular again in recent years.

Comedian Luisa Omielan on stage with her dog Bernie
www.luisaomielan.com

Television and radio

Many different television (TV) channels are available in the UK. Some are free to watch and others require a paid subscription. British television shows a wide variety of programmes. Popular programmes include regular soap operas such as Coronation Street and EastEnders. In Scotland, some Scotland-specific programmes are shown and there is also a channel with programmes in the Gaelic language. There is a Welsh-language channel in Wales. There are also programmes specific to Northern Ireland and some programmes broadcast in Irish Gaelic.

Everyone in the UK with a TV, computer or other medium which can be used for watching TV must have a television licence. One licence covers all of the equipment in one home, except when people rent different rooms in a shared house and each has a separate tenancy agreement – those people must each buy a separate licence. People over 75 can apply for a free TV licence and blind people can get a 50% discount. You will receive a fine of up to £1,000 if you watch TV but do not have a TV licence.

People over 75 do not need a TV licence.

The money from TV licences is used to pay for the British Broadcasting Corporation (BBC). This is a British public service broadcaster providing television and radio programmes. The BBC is the largest broadcaster in the world. It is the only wholly state-funded media organisation that is independent of government. Other UK channels are primarily funded through advertisements and subscriptions.

There are also many different radio stations in the UK. Some broadcast nationally and others in certain cities or regions. There are radio stations that play certain types of music and some broadcast in regional languages such as Welsh or Gaelic. Like television, BBC radio stations are funded by TV licences and other radio stations are funded through advertisements.

Social networking

Social networking websites such as Facebook and Twitter are a popular way for people to stay in touch with friends, organise social events, and share photos, videos and opinions. Many people use social networking on their mobile phones when out and about.

Pubs and night clubs

Public houses (pubs) are an important part of the UK social culture. Many people enjoy meeting friends in the pub. Most communities will have a 'local' pub that is a natural focal point for social activities. Pub quizzes are popular. Pool and darts are traditional pub games. To buy alcohol in a pub or night club you must be 18 or over, but people under that age may be allowed in some pubs with an adult. When they are 16, people can drink wine or beer with a meal in a hotel or restaurant (including eating areas in pubs) as long as they are with someone over 18.

Pubs are usually open during the day from 11.00 am (12 noon on Sundays). Night clubs with dancing and music usually open and close later than pubs. The licensee decides the hours that the pub or night club is open.

Betting and gambling

In the UK, people often enjoy a gamble on sports or other events. There are also casinos in many places. You have to be 18 to go into betting shops or gambling clubs. There is a National Lottery for which draws are made every week. You can enter by buying a ticket or a scratch card. People under 16 are not allowed to participate in the National Lottery.

Minimum age for gambling is 18. For the National Lottery, it is 16.

Pets

A lot of people in the UK have pets such as cats or dogs. They might have them for company or because they enjoy looking after them. It is against the law to treat a pet cruelly or to neglect it. All dogs in public places must wear a collar showing the name and address of the owner. The owner is responsible for keeping the dog under control and for cleaning up after the animal in a public place. Vaccinations and medical treatment for animals are available from veterinary surgeons (vets). There are charities which may help people who cannot afford to pay a vet.

Key points to remember:
- Gardening is a common British pastime.
- Each four countries of the UK have a flower associated to them.
- British film studios have flourished since the 1930s.
- The British film industry hosts its own awards: the BAFTAS.
- Comedy is a regular feature in TV, films and theatre. British humour is renowned.
- The public radio and TV broadcaster, the BBC, is paid for by a public licence.
- Pubs (public houses) are social places to meet for drinks or a meal.
- Gambling and betting are very common.
- Many British families own one or several pets.

7. Places of interest

The UK has a large network of public footpaths in the countryside. There are also many opportunities for mountain biking, mountaineering and hill walking. There are 15 national parks in England, Wales and Scotland. They are areas of protected countryside that everyone can visit, and where people live, work and look after the landscape.

There are many museums in the UK, which range from small community museums to large national and civic collections. Famous landmarks exist in towns, cities and the countryside throughout the UK. Most of them are open to the public to view (generally for a charge).

Many parts of the countryside and places of interest are kept open by the National Trust in England, Wales and Northern Ireland and the National Trust for Scotland. Both are charities that work to preserve important buildings, coastline and countryside in the UK. The National Trust was founded in 1895 by three volunteers. There are now more than 61,000 volunteers helping to keep the organisation running.

UK landmarks

Big Ben is the nickname for the great bell of the clock at the Houses of Parliament in London. Many people call the clock Big Ben as well. The clock is over 150 years old and is a popular tourist attraction. The clock tower is named 'Elizabeth Tower' in honour of Queen Elizabeth II's Diamond Jubilee in 2012.

The Eden Project is located in Cornwall, in the south west of England. Its biomes, which are like giant greenhouses, house plants from all over the world. The Eden Project is also a charity which runs environmental and social projects internationally.

Located on the north-east coast of Northern Ireland, **the Giant's Causeway** is a land formation of columns made from volcanic lava. It was formed about 50 million years ago. There are many legends about the Causeway and how it was formed.

Edinburgh Castle is a dominant feature of the skyline in Scotland. It has a long history, dating back to the early Middle Ages. It is looked after by Historic Environment Scotland, a Scottish government agency.

Loch Lomond and the Trossachs National Park. This national park covers 720 square miles (1,865 square kilometres) in the west of Scotland. Loch Lomond is the largest expanse of fresh water in mainland Britain and probably the best-known part of the park.

Snowdonia is a national park in North Wales. It covers an area of 838 square miles (2,170 square kilometres). Its most well-known landmark is Snowdon, which is the highest mountain in Wales.

The London Eye is situated on the southern bank of the River Thames and is a Ferris wheel that is 443 feet (135 metres) tall. It was originally built as part of the UK's celebration of the new millennium and continues to be an important part of New Year celebrations.

The Tower of London was first built by William the Conqueror after he became king in 1066. Tours are given by the Yeoman Warders, also known as Beefeaters, who tell visitors about the building's history. People can also see the Crown Jewels there.

A modern, thriving society - 7. Places of interest

The Lake District is England's largest national park. It covers 885 square miles (2,292 square kilometres). It is famous for its lakes and mountains and is very popular with climbers, walkers and sailors. The biggest stretch of water is Windermere. In 2007, television viewers voted Wastwater as Britain's favourite view.

UK population

Evolution of British population through the centuries:

Year	Population
1600	4 million
1700	5 million
1801	8 million
1851	20 million
1901	40 million
1951	50 million
1998	57 million
2005	Just under 60 million
2010	Just over 62 million
2019	Over 66.5 million

The population is ageing. There are now a record number of people aged 85 and over.

A modern, thriving society - UK population

Test your knowledge

1. Which famous poem tells the story of the knights at the court of King Arthur?

A. Beowulf

B. Paradise Lost

C. Sir Gawain and the Green Knight

D. King Arthur and his knights

2. Light-hearted plays with music and comedy, which are enjoyed by family audiences and based on fairy stories are known as:

A. Children's plays

B. Pantomimes

C. Hogmanay

D. Parades

3. What is the minimum age requirement in the UK for people to be able to drink wine or beer with a meal in a hotel or restaurant as long as they are with someone over 18?

A. 14 years old

B. 15 years old

C. 16 years old

D. 17 years old

4. Which of the following landmarks is the largest expanse of fresh water in mainland Britain?

A. The River Thames

B. Loch Lomond

C. Loch Ness

D. Lake District

5. Who led the group of Catholics who tried to kill the Protestant king with a bomb in the Houses of the Parliament in 1605?

A. Oliver Cromwell

B. Alexander II

C. Guy Fawkes

D. Adrian IV

A modern, thriving society

6. Who wrote an oratorio called 'Messiah', which is regularly sung by choirs at Easter time?

A. George Frederick Handel
B. Sir Edward Elgar
C. Gustav Holst
D. Henry Purcell

7. What is the most well-known rugby league (club) competition?

A. The Grand National
B. The All England championship
C. The Six Nations championship
D. The Super League

8. Which of the following British poets was inspired by nature?

A. Geoffrey Chaucer
B. William Blake
C. Sir Walter Scott
D. William Wordsworth

9. Where does the most famous sailing event in the UK take place?

A. Holyhead, in North Wales
B. Cowes, in the Isle of Wight
C. Douglas, in the Isle of Man
D. Plymouth, in the South West of England

10. Which TWO British areas have their own banknotes?

A. Northern Ireland
B. Scotland
C. Wales
D. The Isle of Man

Answers: 1.C - 2.B - 3.C - 4.B - 5.C - 6.A - 7.D - 8.D - 9.B - 10.A,B

A modern, thriving society

The UK government, the law and your role

In this chapter you will learn how the UK is governed. You need to understand the King's role in government and his powers. Make sure you understand how people are appointed to the two Houses of Parliament and the specific roles detailed, such as the Speaker and cabinet, and your rights to vote and stand for election. Everyone should understand the workings of the devolved administrations but pay particular attention if you are taking the test in Scotland, Wales or Northern Ireland.

Make sure you know and understand:
- The UK's international role,
- the Commonwealth, EU and other bodies and their member countries,
- common laws, fundamental rights, policing,
- the differences between the various courts and offences,
- taxation, driving and community activity,
- the UK's parliamentary democracy with the monarch as head of state,
- the different institutions which make up this democracy,
- how you can play a part in the democratic process.

1. The development of British democracy

Democracy is a system of government where the whole adult population gets a say. This might be by direct voting or by choosing representatives to make decisions on their behalf. At the turn of the 19th century, Britain was not a democracy as we know it today. Although there were elections to select members of Parliament (MPs), only a small group of people could vote. They were men who were over 21 years of age and who owned a certain amount of property.

The franchise (that is, the number of people who had the right to vote) grew over the course of the 19th century and political parties began to involve ordinary men and women as members.

In the 1830s and 1840s, a group called the Chartists campaigned for reform. They wanted six changes:

- for every man to have the vote
- elections every year
- for all regions to be equal in the electoral system
- secret ballots
- for any man to be able to stand as an MP
- for MPs to be paid.

At the time, the campaign was generally seen as a failure. However, by 1918 most of these reforms had been adopted. The voting franchise was also extended to women over 30, and then in 1928 to men and women over 21. In 1969, the voting age was reduced to 18 for men and women.

Key points to remember:
- The UK is a democracy, a system of government in which the whole adult population can elect their representatives.
- The population allowed to vote is called the franchise.
- Women get equal voting rights to men in 1928.
- Current voting age of 18 was introduced in 1969.

2. The British constitution

A constitution is a set of principles by which a country is governed. It includes all of the institutions that are responsible for running the country and how their power is kept in check. The constitution also includes laws and conventions. The British constitution is not written down in any single document, and therefore it is described as 'unwritten'. This is mainly because the UK, unlike America or France, has never had a revolution which led permanently to a totally new system of government. Our most important institutions have developed over hundreds of years. Some people believe that there should be a single document, but others believe an unwritten constitution allows for more flexibility and better government.

Constitutional institutions

In the UK, there are several different parts of government. The main ones are:

- the monarchy
- Parliament (the House of Commons and the House of Lords)
- the Prime Minister
- the cabinet

- the judiciary (courts)
- the police
- the civil service
- local government.

In addition, there are devolved governments in Scotland, Wales and Northern Ireland that have the power to legislate on certain issues.

The monarchy

King Charles III is the head of state of the UK. He is also the monarch or head of state for many countries in the Commonwealth. The UK has a constitutional monarchy. This means that the king or queen does not rule the country but appoints the government, which the people have chosen in a democratic election. The monarch invites the leader of the party with the largest number of MPs, or the leader of a coalition between more than one party, to become the Prime Minister.

The monarch has regular meetings with the Prime Minister and can advise, warn and encourage, but the decisions on government policies are made by the Prime Minister and cabinet (see The Government p88).

Queen Elizabeth II reigned since her father's death in 1952. In 2012 she celebrated her Diamond Jubilee (60 years as queen) and in 2022, her Platinum Jubilee (70 years of service as queen). She was married to Prince Philip, the Duke of Edinburgh. Her eldest son, Prince Charles (the Prince of Wales) took the throne after her death on the 8th of September 2022.

Queen Elizabeth II died on 8 September 2022 and was succeeded by her son, King Charles III.

The King has important ceremonial roles, such as the opening of the new parliamentary session each year. On this occasion the King makes a speech which summarises the government's policies for the year ahead. All Acts of Parliament are made in his name.

The King represents the UK to the rest of the world. He receives foreign ambassadors and high commissioners, entertains visiting heads of state, and makes state visits overseas in support of diplomatic and economic relationships with other countries. The King has an important role in providing stability and continuity. While governments and Prime Ministers change regularly, the King continues as head of state. He provides a focus for national identity and pride, which is regularly demonstrated through the celebrations of the monarch's Jubilee.

The National Anthem

The National Anthem of the UK is 'God Save the King'. It is played at important national occasions and at events attended by the King or the Royal Family. The first verse is:

'God save our gracious King!
Long live our noble King!
God save the King!
Send him victorious,
Happy and glorious,
Long to reign over us,
God save the King!'

The National Anthem changes its words from Queen to King, depending on the current monarch.

New citizens swear or affirm loyalty to the monarch as part of the citizenship ceremony.

Oath of allegiance	Affirmation of allegiance
'I (name) swear by Almighty God that on becoming a British citizen, I will be faithful and bear true allegiance to His Majesty King Charles the Third, his Heirs and Successors, according to law.'	*'I (name) do solemnly, sincerely and truly declare and affirm that on becoming a British citizen, I will be faithful and bear true allegiance to His Majesty King Charles the Third, his Heirs and Successors, according to law.'*

System of government

The system of government in the UK is a parliamentary democracy. The UK is divided into parliamentary constituencies. Voters in each constituency elect their member of Parliament (MP) in a General Election. All of the elected MPs form the House of Commons. Most MPs belong to a political party, and the party with the majority of MPs forms the government. If one party does not get a majority, two parties can join together to form a coalition.

The House of Commons

The House of Commons is regarded as the more important of the two chambers in Parliament because its members are democratically elected. The Prime Minister and almost all the members of the cabinet are members of the House of Commons (MPs). Each MP represents a parliamentary constituency, which is a small area of the country. MPs have a number of different responsibilities. They:

UK Parliament is formed of two Houses: the Commons, elected and the Lords, appointed

- represent everyone in their constituency
- help to create new laws
- scrutinise and comment on what the government is doing
- debate important national issues.

The House of Lords

Members of the House of Lords, known as peers, are not elected by the people and do not represent a constituency. The role and membership of the House of Lords has changed over the last 50 years.

Westminster Palace, London hosting Parliament and Big Ben
Photo: DaniKauf

Until 1958, all peers were:
- 'hereditary', which means they inherited their title, or
- senior judges, or
- bishops of the Church of England.

Since 1958, the Prime Minister has had the power to nominate peers just for their own lifetime. These are called life peers. They have usually had an important career in politics, business, law or another profession. Life peers are appointed by the monarch on the advice of the Prime Minister. They also include people nominated by the leaders of the other main political parties or by an independent Appointments Commission for non-party peers.

Since 1999, hereditary peers have lost the automatic right to attend the House of Lords. They now elect a few of their number to represent them in the House of Lords.

The House of Lords is normally more independent of the government than the House of

Commons. It can suggest amendments or propose new laws, which are then discussed by MPs. The House of Lords checks laws that have been passed by the House of Commons to ensure they are fit for purpose. It also holds the government to account to make sure that it is working in the best interests of the people. There are peers who are specialists in particular areas, and their knowledge is useful in making and checking laws. The House of Commons has powers to overrule the House of Lords, but these are not used often.

The Speaker

Debates in the House of Commons are chaired by the Speaker. This person is the chief Officer of the House of Commons. The Speaker is neutral and does not represent a political party, even though he or she is an MP, represents a constituency and deals with constituents' problems like any other MP. The Speaker is chosen by other MPs in a secret ballot.

The Speaker keeps order during political debates to make sure the rules are followed. This includes making sure the opposition (see The government) has a guaranteed amount of time to debate issues which it chooses. The Speaker also represents Parliament on ceremonial occasions.

Elections

UK elections

MPs are elected at a General Election, which is held at least every five years. If an MP dies or resigns, there will be a fresh election, called a byelection, in his or her constituency.

MPs are elected through a system called 'first past the post'. In each constituency, the candidate who gets the most votes is elected. The government is usually formed by the party that wins the majority of constituencies. If no party wins a majority, two parties may join together to form a coalition.

European parliamentary elections

Elections for the European Parliament were held every five years. Elected members were called members of the European Parliament (MEPs). Elections to the European Parliament used a system of proportional representation, where seats were allocated to each party in proportion to the total number of votes it has won. Since leaving the European Union, The UK no longer has any MEP.

After the 2016 referendum, the UK left the EU and since 30 Dec 2020 no longer has MEP representation.

Contacting elected members

All elected members have a duty to serve and represent their constituents. You can get contact details for all your representatives and their parties from your local library and from www.parliament.uk. MPs, Assembly members, members of the Scottish Parliament (MSPs) and MEPs are also listed in The Phone Book, published by BT, and in Yellow Pages.

You can contact MPs by letter or telephone at their constituency Office, or at their Office in the House of Commons: The House of Commons, Westminster, London SW1A 0AA, telephone 020 7729 3000. In addition, many MPs, Assembly members, MSPs and MEPs hold regular local 'surgeries', where constituents can go in person to talk about issues that are of concern to them. These surgeries are often advertised in the local newspaper.

Key points to remember:
- The UK doesn't have a written constitution.
- The Monarch is head of state for the UK and several commonwealth nations.
- The Prime Minister and their cabinet take all government decisions.
- The UK is a parliamentary democracy.
- Parliament is made of the House of Commons (where Member of Parliaments are elected during the general elections) and the House of Lords (where Lords and Ladies are appointed.
- Hereditary membership to the House of Lords has stopped since 1999 and hereditary peers now elect their representatives.
- The Speaker of the House manages the debates in the Commons.
- General elections are held every 5 years. British adults have the right to vote.
- The public can contact their MP directly.

3. The government

The Prime Minister
The Prime Minister (PM) is the leader of the political party in power. He or she appoints the members of the cabinet (see below) and has control over many important public appointments. The official home of the Prime Minister is 10 Downing Street, in central

10 Downing Street

London, near the Houses of Parliament. He or she also has a country house outside London called Chequers.

The Prime Minister can be changed if the MPs in the governing party decide to do so, or if he or she wishes to resign. The Prime Minister usually resigns if his or her party loses a General Election.

The cabinet
The Prime Minister appoints about 20 senior MPs to become ministers in charge of departments. These include:
- **Chancellor of the Exchequer** – responsible for the economy
- **Home Secretary** – responsible for crime, policing and immigration
- **Foreign Secretary** – responsible for managing relationships with foreign countries
- Other ministers (called '**Secretaries of State**') responsible for subjects such as education, health and defence.

These ministers form the cabinet, a committee which usually meets weekly and makes important decisions about government policy. Many of these decisions have to be debated or approved by Parliament.

Each department also has a number of other ministers, called Ministers of State and Parliamentary Under-Secretaries of State, who take charge of particular areas of the department's work.

The opposition

The second-largest party in the House of Commons is called the opposition. The leader of the opposition usually becomes Prime Minister if his or her party wins the next General Election.

The leader of the opposition leads his or her party in pointing out what they see as the government's failures and weaknesses. One important opportunity to do this is at Prime Minister's Questions, which takes place every week while Parliament is sitting. The leader of the opposition also appoints senior opposition MPs to be 'shadow ministers'. They form the shadow cabinet and their role is to challenge the government and put forward alternative policies.

The second party after general elections becomes the opposition and forms a shadow cabinet to challenge the government.

The party system

Anyone aged 18 or over can stand for election as an MP but they are unlikely to win unless they have been nominated to represent one of the major political parties. These are the Conservative Party, the Labour Party, the Liberal Democrats, or one of the parties representing Scottish, Welsh or Northern Irish interests.

There are a few MPs who do not represent any of the main political parties. They are called 'independents' and usually represent an issue important to their constituency.

The main political parties actively look for members of the public to join their debates, contribute to their costs, and help at elections for Parliament or for local government. They

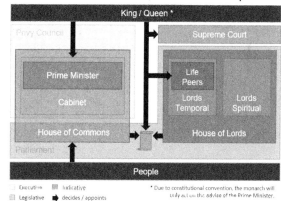

UK Political System - 111Alpha

have branches in most constituencies and hold policy-making conferences every year.

Pressure and lobby groups are organisations which try to influence government policy. They play an important role in politics. Some are representative organisations such as the CBI (Confederation of British Industry), which represents the views of British business. Others campaign on particular topics, such as the environment (for example, Greenpeace) or human rights (for example, Liberty).

The civil service

Civil servants support the government in developing and implementing its policies. They also deliver public services. Civil servants are accountable to ministers. They are chosen on merit and are politically neutral – they are not political appointees. People can apply to join the civil service through an application process, like other jobs in the UK. Civil servants are expected to carry out their role with dedication and a commitment to the civil service and its core values. These are: integrity, honesty, objectivity and impartiality (including being politically neutral).

Local government

Towns, cities and rural areas in the UK are governed by democratically elected councils, often called 'local authorities'. Some areas have both district and county councils, which have different functions. Most large towns and cities have a single local authority. Local authorities provide a range of services in their areas. They are funded by money from central government and by local taxes.

London mayor office
Photo: on_dit

Many local authorities appoint a mayor, who is the ceremonial leader of the council. In some towns, a mayor is elected to be the effective leader of the administration. London has 33 local authorities, with the Greater London Authority and the Mayor of London coordinating policies across the capital. For most local authorities, local elections for councillors are held in May every year. Many candidates stand for council election as members of a political party.

Devolved administrations

Northern Ireland, Scotland and Wales have their own devolved administration.

Since 1997, some powers have been devolved from the central government to give people in Wales, Scotland and Northern Ireland more control over matters that directly affect them. There has been a Welsh Assembly and a Scottish Parliament since 1999. There is also a Northern Ireland Assembly, although this has been suspended on a few occasions.

Policy and laws governing defence, foreign affairs, immigration, taxation and social security all remain under central UK government control. However, many other public services, such as education, are controlled by the devolved administrations. The devolved administrations each have their own civil service.

The Welsh government

The Welsh government and National Assembly for Wales are based in Cardiff, the capital city of Wales. The National Assembly has 60 Assembly members (AMs) and elections are held every four years using a form of proportional representation. Members can speak in either Welsh or English and all of the Assembly's publications are in both languages.

The Assembly has the power to make laws for Wales in 20 areas, including:

- education and training
- health and social services
- economic development
- housing

Since 2011, the National Assembly for Wales has been able to pass laws on these topics without the agreement of the UK Parliament.

The Scottish Parliament

The Scottish Parliament was formed in 1999. It sits in Edinburgh, the capital city of Scotland. There are 129 members of the Scottish Parliament (MSPs), elected by a form of proportional representation. The Scottish Parliament can pass laws for Scotland on all matters which are not specifically reserved to the UK Parliament.

The matters on which the Scottish Parliament can legislate include:

- civil and criminal law
- health
- education
- planning
- additional tax-raising powers.

The Northern Ireland Assembly

A Northern Ireland Parliament was established in 1922, when Ireland was divided, but it was abolished in 1972, shortly after the Troubles broke out in 1969 (see The Partition of Ireland).

The Northern Ireland Assembly was established soon after the Belfast Agreement (or Good Friday Agreement) in 1998. There is a power-sharing agreement which distributes ministerial Offices amongst the main parties. The Assembly has 90 elected members, known as MLAs (members of the Legislative Assembly). They are elected with a form of proportional representation.

The Northern Ireland Assembly can make decisions on issues such as:

- education
- agriculture
- the environment
- health
- social services.

The UK government has the power to suspend all devolved assemblies. It has used this power several times in Northern Ireland when local political leaders found it difficult to work together.

The media and government

Proceedings in Parliament are broadcast on television and published in official reports called Hansard. Written reports can be found in large libraries and at www.parliament.uk. Most people get information about political issues and events from newspapers (often called 'the press'), television, radio and the internet.

The UK has a free press. This means that what is written in newspapers is free from government control. Some newspaper owners and editors hold strong political opinions and run campaigns to try to influence government policy and public opinion. By law, radio and television coverage of the political parties must be balanced and so equal time has to be given to rival viewpoints.

Key points to remember:
- After general elections, the leader of the main party becomes Prime Minister.
- The opposition forms a shadow cabinet to challenge the government.
- Lobby groups exist to try and influence government policies.
- The civil service delivers public services and supports the government to develop and implement policies.
- Local authorities are elected locally to run services in their area.
- Northern Ireland, Scotland and Wales have devolved administrations that can decide their own policies on some topics such as educa Countil tion or health.
- The press in the UK is free. Debates in Parliament can be accessed by the public.
- Parliament proceedings are published through the Hansard report.

4. Who can vote?

The UK has had a fully democratic voting system since 1928 (see The Development of British Democracy). The present voting age of 18 was set in 1969 and (with a few exceptions) all UK-born and naturalised adult citizens have the right to vote.

Adult citizens of the UK, and citizens of the Commonwealth and the Irish Republic who are resident in the UK, can vote in all public elections.

The electoral register

To be able to vote in a parliamentary, local or European election, you must have your name on the electoral register. If you are eligible to vote, you can register by contacting your local council electoral registration Office. This is usually based at your local council (in Scotland it may be based elsewhere). If you don't know which local authority you come under, you can find out by visiting www.aboutmyvote.co.uk and entering your postcode. You can also download voter registration forms in English, Welsh and some other languages.

Members of the public must be registered to vote.

The electoral register is updated every year in September or October. An electoral registration form is sent to every household and this has to be completed and returned with the names of everyone who is resident in the household and eligible to vote.

In Northern Ireland a different system operates. This is called 'individual registration' and all those entitled to vote must complete their own registration form. Once registered, people stay on the register provided their personal details do not change. For more information see the Electoral Office for Northern Ireland website at www.eoni.org.uk

By law, each local authority has to make its electoral register available for anyone to look at, although this has to be supervised. The register is kept at each local electoral registration Office (or council Office in England and Wales). It is also possible to see the register at some public buildings such as libraries.

Where to vote

People vote in elections at places called polling stations, or polling places in Scotland. Before the election you will be sent a poll card. This tells you where your polling station or polling place is and when the election will take place. On election day, the polling station or place will be open from 7.00 am until 10.00 pm.

A polling station in England.
Photo: Philafrenzy

When you arrive at the polling station, the staff will ask for your name and address. In Northern Ireland you will also have to show photographic identification. You will then get your ballot paper, which you take to a polling booth to fill in privately. You should make up your own mind who to vote for. No one has the right to make you vote for a particular candidate. You should follow the instructions on the ballot paper. Once you have completed it, put it in the ballot box. If it is difficult for you to get to a polling station or polling place, you can register for a postal ballot. Your ballot paper will be sent to your home before the election. You then fill it in and post it back. You can choose to do this when you register to vote.

Standing for office

Most citizens of the UK, the Irish Republic or the Commonwealth aged 18 or over can stand for public Office.

There are some exceptions, including:
- members of the armed forces
- civil servants
- people found guilty of certain criminal offences.

Members of the House of Lords may not stand for election to the House of Commons but are eligible for all other public Offices.

Visiting Parliament and the devolved administrations

The UK Parliament

The public can listen to debates in the Palace of Westminster from public galleries in both the House of Commons and the House of Lords.

You can write to your local MP in advance to ask for tickets or you can queue on the day at the public entrance. Entrance is free. Sometimes there are long queues for the House of Commons and people have to wait for at least one to two hours. It is usually easier to get in to the House of Lords. You can find further information on the UK Parliament website at www.parliament.uk.

Northern Ireland Assembly

In Northern Ireland elected members, known as MLAs, meet in the Northern Ireland Assembly at Stormont, in Belfast.

There are two ways to arrange a visit to Stormont. You can either contact the Education Service (details are on the Northern Ireland Assembly website at www.niassembly.gov.uk) or contact an MLA.

Scottish Parliament

In Scotland the elected members, called MSPs, meet in the Scottish Parliament building at Holyrood in Edinburgh (for more information, see www.scottish.parliament.uk).

You can get information, book tickets or arrange tours through visitor services. You can write to them at the Scottish Parliament, Edinburgh, EH99 1SP, telephone 0131 348 5200 or email sp.bookings@scottish.parliament.uk

National Assembly for Wales

In Wales the elected members, known as AMs, meet in the Welsh Assembly in the Senedd in Cardiff Bay (for more information, see www.wales.gov.uk).

The Senedd is an open building. You can book guided tours or seats in the public galleries for the Welsh Assembly. To make a booking, contact the Assembly Booking Service on 0845 010 5500 or email assembly.bookings@wales.gsi.gov.uk.

Key points to remember:

- Adults (over the age of 18) can vote in the UK as long as they have registered on the electoral register and have not been barred (some criminals for instance).
- In Northern Ireland, voters must first complete their 'individual registration'.
- People vote in polling stations, or polling places in Scotland.
- Most people can stand for office (not military or civil servants for example).
- Parliament can devolved administrations are opened to the public for visits.

Northern Ireland

Northern Ireland Assembly
Established June 1998
90 MLA (Members of the Legislative Assembly)
Located at Stormont, in Belfast
Power over:
- education
- agriculture
- the environment
- health
- social services

Stormont Parliamentary Building - Photo: Dom0803

*Edinburgh Scottish Parliament
Photo: or Klaus with K*

Scotland

Scottish Parliament
Established May 1999
129 MSP (Members of the Scottish Parliament)
Located in Holyrood in Edinburgh
Power over:
- civil and criminal law
- health
- education
- planning
- raising taxes

Wales

Welsh Parliament - Senedd
Established May 1999
60 MS (Members of the Senedd)
Located in the Senedd Cardfiff Bay
Power over:
- education and training
- health and social services
- economic development
- housing

Senedd in Cardiff - Photo: UKWiki

5. The UK and international institutions

The Commonwealth

The Commonwealth is an association of countries that support each other and work together towards shared goals in democracy and development. Most member states were once part of the British Empire, although a few countries which were not have also joined. The King is the ceremonial head of the Commonwealth, which currently has 56 member states (see below). Membership is voluntary.

The Commonwealth has no power over its members, although it can suspend membership. The Commonwealth is based on the core values of democracy, good government and the rule of law.

Commonwealth members in 2023

- Antigua and Barbuda
- Australia
- Bahamas, The
- Bangladesh
- Barbados
- Belize
- Botswana
- Brunei Darussalam
- Cameroon
- Canada
- Cyprus
- Dominica
- Fiji
- Gabon
- Gambia
- Ghana
- Grenada
- Guyana
- India
- Jamaica
- Kenya
- Kingdom of Eswatini
- Kiribati
- Lesotho
- Malawi
- Malaysia
- Maldives
- Malta
- Mauritius
- Mozambique
- Namibia
- Nauru
- New Zealand
- Nigeria
- Pakistan
- Papua New Guinea
- Rwanda
- Saint Lucia
- Samoa
- Seychelles
- Sierra Leone
- Singapore
- Solomon Islands
- South Africa
- Sri Lanka
- St Kitts and Nevis
- St Vincent and The Grenadines
- Togo
- Tonga
- Trinidad and Tobago
- Tuvalu
- Uganda
- United Kingdom
- United Republic of Tanzania
- Vanuatu
- Zambia

The European Union

The European Union (EU), originally called the European Economic Community (EEC), was set up by six western European countries (Belgium, France, Germany, Italy, Luxembourg and the Netherlands) who signed the Treaty of Rome on 25 March 1957. The UK originally decided not to join this group but it became a member in 1973. There are now 27 EU member states (see below).

Following the "Brexit" referendum on 23 June 2016, the UK voted to leave the EU. On 31st January 2020, the UK has left the EU.

EU member states in 2023

Austria	France	Malta
Belgium	Germany	Netherlands
Bulgaria	Greece	Poland
Croatia	Hungary	Portugal
Cyprus	Ireland	Romania
Czech Republic	Italy	Slovakia
Denmark	Latvia	Slovenia
Estonia	Lithuania	Spain
Finland	Luxembourg	Sweden

The Council of Europe

The Council of Europe is separate from the EU. It has 46 member countries, including the UK, and is responsible for the protection and promotion of human rights in those countries. It has no power to make laws but draws up conventions and charters, the most well-known of which is the European Convention on Human Rights and Fundamental Freedoms, usually called the European Convention on Human Rights.

In 2023, the UK is NOT a member of the European Union but it IS is member of the Council of Europe.

The United Nations

The UK is part of the United Nations (UN), an international organisation with more than 190 countries as members. The UN was set up after the Second World War and aims to prevent war and promote international peace and security. There are 15 members on the UN Security Council, which recommends action when there are international crises and threats to peace. The UK is one of five permanent members of the Security Council.

UN Security Council room, New York City
Mural painting by Per Krohg

The North Atlantic Treaty Organization (NATO)

The UK is also a member of NATO. NATO is a group of European and North American countries that have agreed to help each other if they come under attack. It also aims to maintain peace between all of its members.

Key points to remember:

- The Commonwealth is mostly formed of countries that were part of the British Empire. The head of the Commonwealth is the King.
- The UK joined the European Union in 1973 and left in 2020.
- The UK remains a member of the Council of Europe and of the European Convention on Human Rights.
- The UK is a member of the United Nations and a permanent member of the UN Security Council.
- The UK is a member of NATO, the North Atlantic Treaty Organization.

6. Respecting the law

One of the most important responsibilities of all residents in the UK is to know and obey the law. This section will tell you about the legal system in the UK and some of the laws that may affect you. Britain is proud of being a welcoming country, but all residents, regardless of their background, are expected to comply with the law and to understand that some things which may be allowed in other legal systems are not acceptable in the UK. Those who do not respect the law should not expect to be allowed to become permanent residents in the UK.

The law is relevant to all areas of life in the UK. You should make sure that you are aware of the laws which affect your everyday life, including both your personal and business affairs.

The law in the UK
Every person in the UK receives equal treatment under the law. This means that the law applies in the same way to everyone, no matter who they are or where they are from.

Laws can be divided into criminal law and civil law:
- Criminal law relates to crimes, which are usually investigated by the police or another authority such as a council, and which are punished by the courts.
- Civil law is used to settle disputes between individuals or groups.

Examples of criminal laws

- **Carrying a weapon:** it is a criminal offence to carry a weapon of any kind, even if it is for self-defence. This includes a gun, a knife or anything that is made or adapted to cause injury.
- **Drugs:** selling or buying drugs such as heroin, cocaine, ecstasy and cannabis is illegal in the UK.
- **Racial crime:** it is a criminal offence to cause harassment, alarm or distress to someone because of their religion or ethnic origin.
- **Selling tobacco:** it is illegal to sell tobacco products (for example, cigarettes, cigars, roll-up tobacco) to anyone under the age of 18.
- **Smoking in public places:** it is against the law to smoke tobacco products in nearly every enclosed public place in the UK. There are signs displayed to tell you where you cannot smoke.
- **Buying alcohol:** it is a criminal offence to sell alcohol to anyone who is under 18 or to buy alcohol for people who are under the age of 18. (There is one exception: people aged 16 or over can drink alcohol with a meal in a hotel or restaurant – see Pubs and Night Clubs.)
- **Drinking in public:** some places have alcohol-free zones where you cannot drink in public. The police can also confiscate alcohol or move young people on from public places. You can be fined or arrested.

This list does not include all crimes. There are many that apply in most countries, such as murder, theft and assault. You can find out more about types of crime in the UK at www.gov.uk

---

Examples of civil laws

- **Housing law:** this includes disputes between landlords and tenants over issues such as repairs and eviction.
- **Consumer rights:** an example of this is a dispute about faulty goods or services.
- **Employment law:** these cases include disputes over wages and cases of unfair dismissal or discrimination in the workplace.
- **Debt:** people might be taken to court if they owe money to someone.

The police and their duties.

The job of the police in the UK is to:
- protect life and property,
- prevent disturbances (also known as keeping the peace),
- prevent and detect crime.

The police are organised into a number of separate police forces headed by Chief Constables. They are independent of the government.

In November 2012, the public elected Police and Crime Commissioners (PCCs) in England and Wales. These are directly elected individuals who are responsible for the delivery of an efficient and effective police force that reflects the needs of their local communities. PCCs set local police priorities and the local policing budget. They also appoint the Chief Constable.

Greater Manchester Police officers
Photo: Terry

The police force is a public service that helps and protects everyone, no matter what their background or where they live. Police Officers must themselves obey the law. They must not misuse their authority, make a false statement, be rude or abusive, or commit racial discrimination. If police Officers are corrupt or misuse their authority they are severely punished.

Police Officers are supported by police community support officers (PSCOs). PSCOs have different roles according to the area but usually patrol the streets, work with the public, and support police Officers at crime scenes and major events.

All people in the UK are expected to help the police prevent and detect crimes whenever they can. If you are arrested and taken to a police station, a police Officer will tell you the reason for your arrest and you will be able to seek legal advice.

If something goes wrong, the police complaints system tries to put it right. Anyone can make a complaint about the police by going to a police station or writing to the Chief Constable of the police force involved. Complaints can also be made to an independent body: the Independent Police Complaints Commission in England and Wales, the Police Complaints Commissioner for Scotland or the Police Ombudsman for Northern Ireland.

Terrorism and extremism

The UK faces a range of terrorist threats. The most serious of these is from Al-Qaeda, its affiliates and like-minded organisations. The UK also faces threats from other kinds of terrorism, such as Northern Ireland-related terrorism.

All terrorist groups try to radicalise and recruit people to their cause. How, where and to what extent they try to do so will vary. Evidence shows that these groups attract very low levels of public support, but people who want to make their home in the UK should be aware of this threat. It is important that all citizens feel safe. This includes feeling safe from all kinds of extremism (vocal or active opposition to fundamental British values), including religious extremism and far-right extremism.

If you think someone is trying to persuade you to join an extremist or terrorist cause, you should notify your local police force.

Key points to remember:
- All residents must comply with the law.
- Criminal law relate to crime for instance selling drugs, drinking in public, racial of other form of abuse, carrying a weapon.
- Civil law is to settle disputes, for instance employment grievance, personal debt or consumer rights.
- There are several forces across the UK, each headed by a Chief Constable.
- Police community support officers assist the police in the local community.
- Members of the public can raise a complaint against the police.

7. The role of the courts

The judiciary

Judges (who are together called 'the judiciary') are responsible for interpreting the law and ensuring that trials are conducted fairly. The government cannot interfere with this.

Sometimes the actions of the government are claimed to be illegal. If the judges agree, then the government must either change its policies or ask Parliament to change the law. If judges find that a public body is not respecting someone's legal rights, they can order that body to change its practices and/or pay compensation. Judges also make decisions in disputes between members of the public or organisations. These might be about contracts, property or employment rights or after an accident.

Criminal courts

There are some differences between the court systems in England and Wales, Scotland and Northern Ireland.

Magistrates' and Justice of the Peace Courts

In England, Wales and Northern Ireland, most minor criminal cases are dealt with in a Magistrates' Court. In Scotland, minor criminal offences go to a Justice of the Peace Court. Magistrates and Justices of the Peace (JPs) are members of the local community. In England, Wales and Scotland they usually work unpaid and do not need legal qualifications. They receive training to do the job and are supported by a legal adviser. Magistrates decide the verdict in each case that comes before them and, if the person is found guilty, the sentence that they are given. In Northern Ireland, cases are heard by a District Judge or Deputy District Judge, who is legally qualified and paid.

Crown Courts and Sheriff Courts

In England, Wales and Northern Ireland, serious offences are tried in front of a judge and a jury in a Crown Court. In Scotland, serious cases are heard in a Sheriff Court with either a sheriff or a sheriff with a jury. The most serious cases in Scotland, such as murder, are heard at a High Court with a judge and jury. A jury is made up of members of the public chosen at random from the local electoral register (see The Electoral Register). In England, Wales and Northern Ireland a jury has 12 members, and in Scotland a jury has 15 members.

Juries in the UK: 12 members except in Scotland: 15 members.

Everyone who is summoned to do jury service must do it unless they are not eligible (for example, because they have a criminal conviction) or they provide a good reason to be excused, such as ill health.

The jury has to listen to the evidence presented at the trial and then decide a verdict of 'guilty' or 'not guilty' based on what they have heard. In Scotland, a third verdict of 'not proven' is also possible. If the jury finds a defendant guilty, the judge decides on the penalty.

Youth Courts

In England, Wales and Northern Ireland, if an accused person is aged 10 to 17, the case is normally heard in a Youth Court in front of up to three specially trained magistrates or a District Judge. The most serious cases will go to the Crown Court. The parents or carers of the young person are expected to attend the hearing. Members of the public are not allowed in Youth Courts, and the name or photographs of the accused young person cannot be published in newspapers or used by the media.

In Scotland a system called the Children's Hearings System is used to deal with children and young people who have committed an offence.

Northern Ireland has a system of youth conferencing to consider how a child should be dealt with when they have committed an offence.

Civil courts

County Courts

County Courts deal with a wide range of civil disputes. These include people trying to get back money that is owed to them, cases involving personal injury, family matters, breaches of contract, and divorce. In Scotland, most of these matters are dealt with in the Sheriff Court. More serious civil cases – for example, when a large amount of compensation is being claimed – are dealt with in the High Court in England, Wales and Northern Ireland. In Scotland, they are dealt with in the Court of Session in Edinburgh.

The small claims procedure

The small claims procedure is an informal way of helping people to settle minor disputes without spending a lot of time and money using a lawyer. This procedure is used for claims of less than £10,000 in England and Wales, £5,000 in Scotland and Northern Ireland. The hearing is held in front of a judge in an ordinary room, and people from both sides of the dispute sit around a table. Small claims can also be issued online through Money Claims Online (www.moneyclaim.gov.uk).

> *Small claim limits*
> *England and Wales:*
> *£10.000*
> *Scotland and N. Ireland: £5.000*

You can get details about the small claims procedure from your local County Court or Sheriff Court.

Details of your local court can be found as follows: England and Wales: at www.gov.uk

- Scotland: at www.scotcourts.gov.uk
- Northern Ireland: at www.courtsni.gov.uk

(Note: *Be careful as the limits on small claims does change quite often.*)

Legal advice

Solicitors

Solicitors are trained lawyers who give advice on legal matters, take action for their clients and represent their clients in court.

There are solicitors' Offices throughout the UK. It is important to find out which aspects of law a solicitor specialises in and to check that they have the right experience to help you with your case. Many advertise in local newspapers and in Yellow Pages.

The Citizens Advice Bureau (www.citizensadvice.org.uk) can give you names of local solicitors and which areas of law they specialise in. You can also get this information from the Law Society (www.lawsociety.org.uk) in England and Wales, the Law Society of Scotland (www.lawscot.org.uk) or the Law Society of Northern Ireland (www.lawsoc-ni.org).

Solicitors' charges are usually based on how much time they spend on a case. It is very important to find out at the start how much a case is likely to cost.

Key points to remember:

- The judiciary is independent from the government and ensures the fairness of trials.
- The criminal justice system varies between the members of the UK.
- Small claim limits vary across the UK.
- Solicitors are professionally trained lawyers that can advise on legal matters.
- The Citizen Advice Bureau can give initial advice and give details of solicitors.

Criminal courts across the UK - a comparison chart

	England	Wales	N. Ireland	Scotland
Minor Criminal Cases	Magistrates Court			Justice of Peace Court
	Magistrates *(Unpaid but trained members of public)*		District Judges *(Legally qualified and paid)*	Justices of Peace *(Unpaid but trained members of public)*
Serious cases	Crown Court			Sheriff Court
	Judge *(Paid professionals)* + Jury *(12 members of the public)*			Sheriff *(Law professional, appointed)* + Jury *(15 members of the public)*
Very serious crime	Crown Court			High Court
	Judge *(Paid professionals)* + Jury *(12 members of the public)*			Judge *(Professional)* + Jury *(15 members of the public)*
Accused is under 18	Youth Court			Children's Hearing System
	Magistrates *(Unpaid but specially trained members of public)*		District Judges *(Legally qualified and paid)*	3 x Panel members *(Specially trained members of public)* If it goes to court: Sheriff

8. Fundamental principles

Britain has a long history of respecting an individual's rights and ensuring essential freedoms. These rights have their roots in Magna Carta, the Habeas Corpus Act and the Bill of Rights of 1689 (see Legal and Political Changes, The Restoration and Constitutional Monarchy – A Bill of Rights), and they have developed over a period of time. British diplomats and lawyers had an important role in drafting the European Convention on Human Rights and Fundamental Freedoms. The UK was one of the first countries to sign the Convention in 1950.

Some of the principles included in the European Convention on Human Rights are:
- right to life
- prohibition of torture
- prohibition of slavery and forced labour
- right to liberty and security
- right to a fair trial
- freedom of thought, conscience and religion
- freedom of expression (speech).

The Human Rights Act 1998 incorporated the European Convention on Human Rights into UK law. The government, public bodies and the courts must follow the principles of the Convention.

Equal opportunities

UK laws ensure that people are not treated unfairly in any area of life or work because of their age, disability, sex, pregnancy and maternity, race, religion or belief, sexuality or marital status. If you face problems with discrimination, you can get more information from the Citizens Advice Bureau or from one of the following organisations:

- England and Wales: Equality and Human Rights Commission (www.equalityhumanrights.com)
- Scotland: Equality and Human Rights Commission in Scotland (www.equalityhumanrights.com/scotland/the-commission-inscotland) and Scottish Human Rights Commission (www.scottishhumanrights.com)
- Northern Ireland: Equality Commission for Northern Ireland (www.equalityni.org)
- Northern Ireland Human Rights Commission (www.nihrc.org).

Domestic violence

In the UK, brutality and violence in the home is a serious crime. Anyone who is violent towards their partner – whether they are a man or woman, married or living together – can be prosecuted. Any man who forces a woman to have sex, including a woman's husband, can be charged with rape.

It is important for anyone facing domestic violence to get help as soon as possible. A solicitor or the Citizens Advice Bureau can explain the available options. In some areas there are safe places to go and stay in, called refuges or shelters.

There are emergency telephone numbers in the helpline section at the front of Yellow Pages, including, for women, the number of the nearest women's centre. You can also phone the 24-hour National Domestic Violence Freephone Helpline on 0808 2000 247 at any time, or the police can help you find a safe place to stay.

Female genital mutilation
Female genital mutilation (FGM), also known as cutting or female circumcision, is illegal in the UK. Practising FGM or taking a girl or woman abroad for FGM is a criminal offence.

Forced marriage
A marriage should be entered into with the full and free consent of both people involved. Arranged marriages, where both parties agree to the marriage, are acceptable in the UK. Forced marriage is where one or both parties do not or cannot give their consent to enter into the partnership. Forcing another person to marry is a criminal offence.

Forced Marriage Protection Orders were introduced in 2008 for England, Wales and Northern Ireland under the Forced Marriage (Civil Protection) Act 2007. Court orders can be obtained to protect a person from being forced into a marriage, or to protect a person in a forced marriage. Similar Protection Orders were introduced in Scotland in November 2011.

A potential victim, or someone acting for them, can apply for an order. Anyone found to have breached an order can be jailed for up to two years for contempt of court.

Key points to remember:
- The UK has a long history of protecting rights (Habeas Corpus, Bill of Rights).
- The UK is a founder of the European Convention on Human Rights.
- Nobody should face discrimination in the UK because of sex, race, belief, sexuality, disability etc.
- Domestic violence is a serious crime in the UK.
- Forced marriage, forced sex, forced mutilation are all illegal in the UK.
- Anyone in a situation of abuse can contact the Citizens Advice Bureau or seek legal advice from a solicitor.

9. Taxation

Income tax

People in the UK have to pay tax on their income, which includes:

- wages from paid employment
- profits from self-employment
- taxable benefits
- pensions
- income from property, savings and dividends.

Money raised from income tax pays for government services such as roads, education, police and the armed forces.

For most people, the right amount of income tax is automatically taken from their income from employment by their employer and paid directly to HM Revenue & Customs (HMRC), the government department that collects taxes. This system is called 'Pay As You Earn' (PAYE). If you are self-employed, you need to pay your own tax through a system called 'self-assessment', which includes completing a tax return. Other people may also need to complete a tax return. If HMRC sends you a tax return, it is important to complete and return the form as soon as you have all the necessary information.

You can find out more about income tax at www.hmrc.gov.uk/incometax. You can get help and advice about taxes and completing tax forms from the HMRC self-assessment helpline, on 0845 300 0627, and the HMRC website at www.hmrc.gov.uk.

National insurance

Almost everybody in the UK who is in paid work, including self-employed people, must pay National Insurance Contributions. The money raised from National Insurance Contributions is used to pay for state benefits and services such as the state retirement pension and the National Health Service (NHS).

Employees have their National Insurance Contributions deducted from their pay by their employer. People who are self-employed need to pay National Insurance Contributions themselves. Anyone who does not pay enough National Insurance Contributions will not be able to receive certain contributory benefits such as Jobseeker's Allowance or a full state retirement pension. Some workers, such as part-time workers, may not qualify for statutory payments such as maternity pay if they do not earn enough.

Further guidance about National Insurance Contributions is available on HMRC's website at www.hmrc.gov.uk/ni.

Getting a National Insurance number

A National Insurance number is a unique personal account number. It makes sure that the National Insurance Contributions and tax you pay are properly recorded against your name. All young people in the UK are sent a National Insurance number just before their 16th birthday.

A non-UK national living in the UK and looking for work, starting work or setting up as self-employed will need a National Insurance number. However, you can start work without one. If you have permission to work in the UK, you will need to telephone the Department for Work and Pensions (DWP) to arrange to get a National Insurance number. You may be required to attend an interview. The DWP will advise you of the appropriate application process and tell you which documents you will need to bring to an interview if one is necessary. You will usually need documents that prove your identity and that you have permission to work in the UK. A National Insurance number does not on its own prove to an employer that you have the right to work in the UK.

You can find out more information about how to apply for a National Insurance number at www.gov.uk.

Key points to remember:
- Tax from employment is taken at the source through a system called Pay As You Earn or PAYE - meaning the money you receive from work is fully yours.
- Anyone working in the UK should have a National Insurance Number and pay the relevant National Insurance Contribution on their salary.
- It is possible to start working without a National Insurance number by contacting the Department of Work and Pension who will advise on the process.

10. Driving

In the UK, you must be at least 17 years old to drive a car or motor cycle and you must have a driving licence to drive on public roads. To get a UK driving licence you must pass a driving test, which tests both your knowledge and your practical skills. You need to be at least 16 years old to ride a moped, and there are other age requirements and special tests for driving large vehicles.

Drivers can use their driving licence until they are 70 years old. After that, the licence is valid for three years at a time.

Learning drivers must display a red 'L' plate (for learner) on their car until they receive their full licence. In Northern Ireland, a newly qualified driver must display an 'R' place (for restricted driver) for one year after passing the test.

If your driving licence is from a country in the European Union (EU), Iceland, Liechtenstein or Norway, you can drive in the UK for 12 months after your arrival. If you have a licence from any other country, you may use it in the UK for up to 12 months. To continue driving after that, you must get a UK full driving licence.

If you are resident in the UK, your car or motor cycle must be registered at the Driver and Vehicle Licensing Agency (DVLA). You must pay an annual road tax . You must also have valid motor insurance. It is a serious criminal offence to drive without insurance. If your vehicle is over three years old, you must take it for a Ministry of Transport (MOT) test every year. It is an offence not to have an MOT certificate if your vehicle is more than three years old. You can find out more about vehicle tax and MOT requirements from www.gov.uk.

Key points to remember:
- Individuals can start driving from the age of 17.
- Once a driver reaches 70 years old, they must renew their licence every 3 years.
- Drivers from other countries can drive for up 12 months under their non UK licence and can exchange it during that time for a UK licence.
- Car owners must pay tax road and car insurance
- Cars older than three years must pass an annual test from the Ministry of Transport called the MOT test.

11. Your role in the community

Becoming a British citizen or settling permanently in the UK brings responsibilities but also opportunities. Everyone has the opportunity to participate in their community. This section looks at some of the responsibilities of being a citizen and gives information about how you can help to make your community a better place to live and work.

Values and responsibilities
Although Britain is one of the world's most diverse societies, there is a set of shared values and responsibilities that everyone can agree with.

These values and responsibilities include:
- to obey and respect the law
- to be aware of the rights of others and respect those rights
- to treat others with fairness
- to behave responsibly
- to help and protect your family
- to respect and preserve the environment
- to treat everyone equally, regardless of sex, race, religion, age, disability, class or sexual orientation
- to work to provide for yourself and your family
- to help others
- to vote in local and national government elections.

Taking on these values and responsibilities will make it easier for you to become a full and active citizen.

Being a good neighbour

When you move into a new house or apartment, introduce yourself to the people who live near you. Getting to know your neighbours can help you to become part of the community and make friends. Your neighbours are also a good source of help – for example, they may be willing to feed your pets if you are away, or offer advice on local shops and services.

You can help prevent any problems and conflicts with your neighbours by respecting their privacy and limiting how much noise you make. Also try to keep your garden tidy, and only put your refuse bags and bins on the street or in communal areas if they are due to be collected.

Getting involved in local activities

Volunteering and helping your community are an important part of being a good citizen. They enable you to integrate and get to know other people. It helps to make your community a better place if residents support each other. It also helps you to fulfil your duties as a citizen, such as behaving responsibly and helping others.

Key points to remember:
- All British citizens share similar values to leave together in harmony.
- Neighbours can be a source of help, make sure you know yours.
- Many get involved in their local community through volunteering.

12. How you can support your community

There are a number of positive ways in which you can support your community and be a good citizen.

Jury service

As well as getting the right to vote, people on the electoral register are randomly selected to serve on a jury. Anyone who is on the electoral register and is aged 18 to 70 can be asked to do this.

Helping in schools

If you have children, there are many ways in which you can help at their schools. Parents can often help in classrooms, by supporting activities or listening to children read.

Many schools organise events to raise money for extra equipment or out-of-school activities. Activities might include book sales, toy sales or bringing food to sell. You might have good ideas of your own for raising money. Sometimes events are organised by parent-teacher associations (PTAs). Volunteering to help with their events or joining the association is a way of doing something good for the school and also making new friends in your local community. You can find out about these opportunities from notices in the school or notes your children bring home.

School governors and school boards

School governors, or members of the school board in Scotland, are people from the local community who wish to make a positive contribution to children's education. They must be aged 18 or over at the date of their election or appointment. There is no upper age limit.

Governors and school boards have an important part to play in raising school standards. They have three key roles:
- setting the strategic direction of the school
- ensuring accountability
- monitoring and evaluating school performance.
- You can contact your local school to ask if they need a new governor or school board member. In England, you can also apply online at the School Governors' One-Stop Shop at www.sgoss.org.uk. In England, parents and other community groups can apply to open a free school in their local area. More information about this can be found on the Department for Education website at www.dfe.gov.uk.

Supporting political parties

Political parties welcome new members. Joining one is a way to demonstrate your support for certain views and to get involved in the democratic process.

Political parties are particularly busy at election times. Members work hard to persuade people to vote for their candidates – for instance, by handing out leaflets in the street or by knocking on people's doors and asking for their support. This is called 'canvassing'. You don't have to tell a canvasser how you intend to vote if you don't want to.

British citizens can stand for Office as a local councillor, a member of Parliament (or the devolved equivalents). This is an opportunity to become even more involved in the political life of the UK. You may also be able to stand for Office if you are an Irish citizen or an eligible Commonwealth citizen or.

You can find out more about joining a political party from the individual party websites.

Helping with local services

There are opportunities to volunteer with a wide range of local service providers, including local hospitals and youth projects. Services often want to involve local people in decisions about the way in which they work. Universities, housing associations, museums and arts councils may advertise for people to serve as volunteers in their governing bodies.

You can volunteer with the police, and become a special constable or a lay (non-police) representative. You can also apply to become a magistrate. You will often find advertisements for vacancies in your local newspaper or on local radio. You can also find out more about these sorts of roles at www.gov.uk.

Blood and organ donation

Donated blood is used by hospitals to help people with a wide range of injuries and illnesses. Giving blood only takes about an hour to do. You can register to give blood at:

- England and North Wales: www.blood.co.uk
- Rest of Wales: www.welsh-blood.org.uk
- Scotland: www.scotblood.co.uk
- Northern Ireland: www.nibts.org

Many people in the UK are waiting for organ transplants. All adults in England are now considered to have agreed to be an organ donor when they die unless they have recorded a decision not to donate or are in one of the excluded groups.

Other ways to volunteer

Volunteering is working for good causes without payment. There are many benefits to volunteering, such as meeting new people helping make your community a better place. Some volunteer activities will give you a chance to practise your English or develop work skills that will help you find a job or improve your curriculum vitae (CV). Many people volunteer simply because they want to help other people.

Activities you can do as a volunteer include:
- working with animals – for example, caring for animals at a local rescue shelter
- youth work – for example, volunteering at a youth group
- helping improve the environment – for example, participating in a litter pick-up in the local area
- working with the homeless in, for example, a homelessness shelter
- mentoring – for example, supporting someone who has just come out of prison
- work in health and hospitals – for example, working on an information desk in a hospital
- helping older people at, for example, a residential care home.

There are thousands of active charities and voluntary organisations in the UK. They work to improve the lives of people, animals and the environment in many different ways. They range from the British branches of international organisations, such as the British Red Cross, to small local charities working in particular areas. They include charities working with older people (such as Age UK), with children (for example, the National Society for the Prevention of Cruelty to Children (NSPCC)), and with the homeless (for example, Crisis and Shelter).

There are also medical research charities (for example, Cancer Research UK), environmental charities (including the National Trust and Friends of the Earth) and charities working with animals (such as the People's Dispensary for Sick Animals (PDSA)).

Volunteers are needed to help with their activities and to raise money. The charities often advertise in local newspapers, and most have websites that include information about their opportunities. You can also get information about volunteering for different organisations from www.do-it.org.uk.

There are many opportunities for young people to volunteer and receive accreditation which will help them to develop their skills. These include the National Citizen Service programme, which gives 16- and 17-year-olds the opportunity to enjoy outdoor activities, develop their skills and take part in a community project. You can find out more about these opportunities as follows:
- National Citizen Service: at nationalcitizenservice.direct.gov.uk
- England: at www.vinspired.com
- Wales: at www.gwirvol.org
- Scotland: at www.vds.org.uk
- Northern Ireland: at www.volunteernow.co.uk

Looking after the environment
It is important to recycle as much of your waste as you can. Using recycled materials to make new products uses less energy and means that we do not need to extract more raw materials from the earth. It also means that less rubbish is created, so the amount being put into landfill is reduced.

You can learn more about recycling and its benefits at www.recyclenow.com. At this website you can also find out what you can recycle at home and in the local area if you live in England. This information is available:
- for Wales at www.wasteawarenesswales.org.uk
- for Scotland at www.recycleforscotland.com
- and for Northern Ireland from your local authority.

A good way to support your local community is to shop for products locally where you can. This will help businesses and farmers in your area and in Britain. It will also reduce your carbon footprint, because the products you buy will not have had to travel as far.

Walking and using public transport to get around when you can is also a good way to protect the environment. It means that you create less pollution than when you use a car.

Key points to remember:
- There are many ways through which citizens can support their community.
- Assist schools through fund raising and by becoming a governor.
- Get involved in politics, help parties in canvassing.
- Join a charity or a volunteering organisations.

Test your knowledge

1. Members of the European Parliament (MEPs) are elected on the basis of:
A.   Personal achievements
B.   Instant run-off
C.   First past the post system (the candidate who gets the most votes)
D.   Proportional representation

2. The House of Commons is normally more independent of the government than the House of Lords:
A.   True
B.   False

3. Who is the ceremonial head of the Commonwealth?
A.   The British Queen
B.   The Pope
C.   The President of the United States
D.   The Prime Minister of the UK

4. On which of the following issues the Northern Ireland Assembly CANNOT make decisions?
A.   Health
B.   Education
C.   The Environment
D.   Planning

5. What was celebrated at the Diamond Jubilee in 2012?
A.   60 years of Elizabeth II as Queen
B.   50 years of Elizabeth II as Queen
C.   The Olympic Games taking place in the UK
D.   The success of the British poetry

6. Who is responsible for managing relationships with foreign countries?
A.   The Chancellor of the Exchequer
B.   The Foreign Secretary
C.   The Home Secretary
D.   The Queen

7. Which of the following is NOT a devolved administration?

A. The Scottish Parliament
B. The Welsh Assembly
C. The Irish Parliament
D. The Northern Ireland Assembly

8. Which TWO of the following charities work with homeless people?

A. Friends of the Earth
B. Shelter
C. Crisis
D. Oxfam

9. Which of the following is a criminal offence?

A. Selling tobacco to someone under the age of 18
B. Owing money to someone
C. Discrimination in the workplace
D. Selling faulty goods or services

10. Which Court deals with the most serious civil cases in England, Wales and Northern Ireland?

A. The County Court
B. The Crown Court
C. The High Court
D. The Sheriff Court

The UK government, the law and your role

REVISION

British monarchs

This is the chronological order of all monarchs in the UK. The third column provides some information about their connection to the previous monarch.

English Kings

Dates	Name	Relationship to previous
827 - 839	EGBERT	First monarch
839-856	AETHELWULF	Son
856 - 860	AETHELBALD	Son
860 - 866	AETHELBERT	Brother
866 - 871	AETHELRED I	Brother
871 - 899	ALFRED THE GREAT	Son
924 - 939	ATHELSTAN	Son
939 - 946	EDMUND	Half brother
946 - 955	EADRED	Son of Edward the Elder
955 - 959	EADWIG	Son of Edmund I
959 - 975	EDGAR	Son of Edmund I
975 - 978	EDWARD THE MARTYR	Son
978 - 1016	AETHELRED II THE UNREADY	Son of Edgar
1016 - 1016	EDMUND II IRONSIDE	Son
1016 - 1035	Canute the Dane aka Cnut the great	New line
1035 - 1040	HAROLD I	Illegitimate son of Canute
1040 - 1042	HARTHACANUTE	Son of Canute
1042-1066	EDWARD THE CONFESSOR	Half brother
1066	HAROLD II	Not related

Norman Kings

Dates	Name	Relationship to previous
1066- 1087	WILLIAM I	The Conqueror - Duke of Normandy, invaded England
1087- 1100	WILLIAM II	Son
1100-1135	HENRY I	Son of William I
1135-1154	Stephen	Grandson of William I

Plantagenet Kings

Dates	Name	Relationship to previous
1154-1189	HENRY II	New line
1189 - 1199	RICHARD I	Son of Henry II - Lionheart
1199 -1216	John	Son of Henry II
1216 -1272	HENRY III	Son of John

Monarchs of England and Wales

Dates	Name	Relationship to previous
1272 - 1307	EDWARD I	Son of Henry III
1307 - 1327	EDWARD II	Son - *deposed*
1327 - 1377	EDWARD III	Son
1377 - 1399	RICHARD II	Grandson of Edward III - *deposed*

House of Lancaster

Dates	Name	Relationship to previous
1399 - 1413	HENRY IV	Grandson of Edward III
1413 - 1422	HENRY V	Son
1422 - 1461	HENRY VI	Son

House of York

Dates	Name	Relationship to previous
1461- 1483	EDWARD IV	Grandson of Henry VI
1483 - 1483	EDWARD V	Son
1483 - 1485	RICHARD III	Brother of Edward IV

The Tudors

Dates	Name	Relationship to previous
1485 - 1509	HENRY VII	New dynasty
1509 - 1547	HENRY VIII	Son
1547 - 1553	EDWARD VI	Son
1553 - 1558	MARY I	Daughter of Henry VIII (Bloody Mary)
1558-1603	ELIZABETH I	Daughter of Henry VIII

The Stuarts

Dates	Name	Relationship to previous
1603-1625	JAMES I and VI of Scotland	Son of Mary Queen of Scots
1625 - 1649	CHARLES 1	Son

The Commonwealth

Dates	Name	Relationship to previous
1653 - 1658	OLIVER CROMWELL	Lord Protector not King
1658 - 1659	RICHARD CROMWELL	Son - Lord Protector not King

The Restoration

Dates	Name	Relationship to previous
1660 - 1685	CHARLES II	Son of Charles I
1685 - 1688	JAMES II and VII of Scotland	Son of Charles I and brother to Charles II
1689 - 1702	WILLIAM III and Mary II	Grandson of Charles I
1702 - 1714	ANNE	Daughter of James II

The Hanoverians

Dates	Name	Relationship to previous
1714-1727	GEORGE I	Great Grandson of James I
1727 - 1760	GEORGE II	Son
1760 - 1820	GEORGE III	Grandson of George II
1820 - 1830	GEORGE IV	Son
1830 - 1837	WILLIAM IV	Brother
1837 - 1901	VICTORIA	Grand-daughter of George III
1901 - 1910	EDWARD VII	Son

House of Windsor

Dates	Name	Relationship to previous
1910 - 1936	GEORGE V	Brother
1936	EDWARD VIII	Son - Abdicated
1936 - 1952	GEORGE VI	Brother
1952-	ELIZABETH II	daughter

The UK government, the law and your role - The Stuarts

Key Dates

This is a list in chronological order of the key dates in the official book. You don't need to know all of them for the test but you should have a good overall knowledge of the main period and when key events took place.

Year	Event
8000BC	Channel forms. England is separated from Europe
4000BC	First farmers arrive in Britain
2000BC	Bronze Age
55BC	Julius Caesar and the Romans fail to invade Britain
43AD	The romans successfully invade Britain
122AD	Hadrian's wall construction begins
410AD	The Roman army leaves
600	Anglo-Saxon kingdoms are established
789	The Vikings first come to Britain
1066	Battle of Hastings William of Normandy invade Britain
1215	Magna Carta makes the King subject to the Law
1284	King Edward I annexes Wales to England (Statute of Rhuddlan)
1314	Robert the Bruce leads the Scottish to victory against the English at the battle of Bannockburn
1348	The Black Death kills a third of population
1415	Battle of Agincourt: victory against the French and end of the Hundred Year War.
1455	Wars of the Roses begin between Houses of York and Lancaster
1485	Battle of Bosworth: King Richard III is killed by Henry Tudor of Lancaster. End of the Wars of Roses. Henry Tudor becomes King Henry VII
1560	Scottish Parliament abolishes the authority of the Pope and makes Roman Catholic service illegal
1588	Victory over the Spanish Armada
1603	Death of Elizabeth I. Her cousin, King James I succeeds her.
1641	Start of a rebellion in Ireland
1642	Civil war between King Charles I and the Parliament.
1646	Parliament wins and holds Charles I prisoner
1649	Charles I is executed
1656	Jews settle in London
1658	Death of Oliver Cromwell

1660	Parliament asks Charles II to come back from Exile
1665	Major outbreak of Plague in London
1666	Big fire of London
1679	Habeas Corpus. No one can be held prisoner unlawfully.
1685	Charles II's death. His brother becomes King James II of England and King James VII of Scotland
1688	Protestants ask William of Orange to invade England. There is little resistance. (Glorious Revolution).
1689	The Bill of Rights confirms the rights of Parliament and limits the King's power. Monarch must be Protestant and Parliament is elected every 3 years
1690	William defeats James II at the battle of the Boyne in Ireland.
1680-1720	Huguenots immigration. They are refugees from France.
1707	The Act of Union creates the Kingdom of Great Britain
1714	Queen Anne dies and George I becomes King
1721-1742	First Prime Minister in exercise: Sir Robert Walpole
1745	Charles Edward Stuart attempts to take the throne to restore the Stuart dynasty
1746	Battle of Culloden: George II wins against Charles Stuart. Scottish clans lose their power
Late 1700s	Quakers group oppose slavery
1776	13 colonies in America declare their independence
1783	Britain recognises the American colonies independence
1789	Revolution in France. France declares war on Britain
1801	The Act of Union creates the United Kingdom of Great Britain and Ireland. The Union Flag is created (called Union Jack)
1805	Victory against France at Trafalgar. Admiral Nelson is killed during the battle
1807	It becomes illegal to trade slaves on British ships
1815	End of the French Wars with the victory at Waterloo. Napoleon defeated by the Duke of Wellington (the Iron Duke)
1832	The Reform Act increases the number of people allowed to vote
1833	The Emancipation Act abolishes slavery. 2 million Chinese and Indians are employed to replace slaves
1837	Victoria becomes Queen
1846	Repealing of the Corn Laws opens up import

1847	Women and children working hours are limited to 10 hours per day
1853-1856	Crimean War against Russia
1867	Second Reform Act creates urban seats in Parliament and reduces the wealth needed to be allowed to vote
1870	Act of Parliament for married women allows them to keep their earnings
1882	Second act of Parliament for married women allows them to own their own property
1899-1902	The Boer War in South Africa against settlers from Netherland called Boers.
1913	Home Rule Bill for Ireland proposes Ireland to have its own parliament. It is opposed by protestants from North Ireland
1914	The Archduke Franz Ferdinand of Austria is assassinated. This starts World War I
1916	Battle of the Somme killed about 60,000 soldiers in just one day
1916	The Easter Rising, Irish Nationalist rise against the British in Dublin
1918	At 11.00 am on the 11th November, the war ends with victory for Britain and allies
1921	Peace treaty for Ireland
1922	Ireland becomes 2 countries. Northern Ireland is created. The rest of Ireland becomes a free state
1922	First BBC radio broadcast
1929	Great Depression: mass unemployment
1933	Hitler comes to power in Germany
1936	First BBC Television broadcast
1939	Germany invades Poland. The UK and France declare wars on Germany. This starts World War II
1940	German forces win over the allies and advance through France. Churchill becomes Prime Minister. Dunkirk operation where the Navy rescues more than 300,000 men from beaches in France. Creates the "Dunkirk Spirit" The Battle of Britain is fought in the air to prevent German invasion
1941	Germany invades the Soviet Union The Japanese attack Pearl Harbour in the US. The USA join the allied forces and the war becomes fully global
1944	6 June: the allied forces land in French Normandy (the D-Day) and start repelling the German.

1945	Germany is defeated by the allies. 8 May: Victory in Europe and Germany surrenders August: The US drop 2 atomic bombs over Japanese cities, Hiroshima and Nagasaki to end the war. A Labour government is elected. Clement Attlee becomes Prime Minister
1947	Several countries gain independence from the British Empire: India, Pakistan, Ceylon
1948	The Minister the Health Aneurin Bevan creates the National Health Service (NHS)
1949	Ireland becomes a republic with its own government
1951	Churchill becomes Prime Minister again
1950s	Shortage of labour leads to vast immigration
1957	The European Economic Community is formed by Germany, France, Italy, Belgium, Luxemburg and the Netherlands.
1960s	The Swinging Sixties are a period of social changes., many laws are liberalised (divorce and abortion). Women's position in the workplace improves Technological progress. France and the UK develop a supersonic airliner called Concorde. Immigration laws are enforced to reduce flows.
1970s	End of prosperity. Imports become more expensive than exports. Difficulties between Trade Unions and government.
1972	Northern Ireland Parliament is suspended and the UK government rules over the country. Unrest and violence in Ireland lasts several decades
1973	The UK joins the European Economic Community
1997	Tony Blair is elected Labour Prime Minister
1998	The Good Friday Agreement restores peace in Ireland
1999	Welsh Assembly and a Scottish Parliament are created
2000	British troops fight in Iraq alongside the USA.
2010	A coalition government is formed by the Conservatives and the Liberal Democrats. David Cameron is Prime Minister and Nick Clegg his deputy
2015	David Cameron remains Prime minister
2016	Following a referendum to leave the European Union, David Cameron resigns and Theresa May becomes Prime Minister
2017	The UK triggers article 50 of the Treaty of Lisbon to initiate its departure from the European Union.
2020	On 31 January, the UK leaves the European Union.

Important people

The six wives of Henry VIII:
- **Catherine of Aragon** – Spanish princess. One children survived: Mary. Henry divorced her, leading to a split with the Catholic Church
- **Anne Boleyn** – English. They have one daughter, Elizabeth. Accused of cheating, she was executed.
- **Jane Seymour** – English. They have a son: Edward. She died shortly after his birth
- **Anne of Cleves** – German princess. Political marriage that didn't last.
- **Catherine Howard** – Cousin of Anne Boleyn. Also accused of cheating and executed.
- **Catherine Parr** – Widow. Died shortly after Henry

William Shakespeare (1564 – 1616)
Born in Stratford-Upon-Avon. Playwright and actor, famous for many plays including *Romeo and Juliet, Hamlet, Macbeth, A Midsummer's night dream.* He largely influenced English language and invented many words (critic, lonely, swager, unearthly, unreal.)

Isaac Newton (1643-1727)
Born in Lincolnshire, studied at Cambridge University. Scientist famous for his book *Philosophiae Naturalis Principia Mathematica* which demonstrated the laws of gravity.

Robert Burns (1759-1796)
Scottish poet known as 'The Bard' who wrote in Scots. Famous song: *Auld Lang Syne.*

Richard Arkwright (1732-1792)
Trained as a barber and started to work in textiles. He improved the machine that prepares fibres and developed a horse-driven spinning mill before replacing horses with a steam engine. He is famous for running efficient and profitable factories.

Sake Dean Mahomet (1759-1851)
Born in Bengal, India. He served the Bengal army and moved to Britain in 1782. He opened the first curry house in London and for introduced shampooing to Britain.

Isambard Kingdom Brunel (1806-1859)
Born in Portsmouth, trained in France, he was an engineer. Famous for building the Great Western Railway as well as many bridges, tunnels and ships.

Florence Nightingale (1820-1910)
Born in Italy, trained as a nurse, she went to work in Turkish hospitals during the Crimean war. She is famous for improving the conditions in hospitals and creating training schools for nurses at St Thomas' Hospital in London.

Emmeline Pankhurst (1858-1928)
Born in Manchester, she set up the Women's Franchise League in 1889 to fight for women's right to vote. She founded the women's Social and Political Union (WSPU) also called the suffragettes. In 1918, they won the right to vote for women over 30.

Rudyard Kipling (1865-1936)
Born in India, he wrote poems and books. Most famous for the Jungle Book and the poem If. He won the Noble prize for literature in 1907.

Winston Churchill (1874-1965)
Became a Conservative MP in 1900. In May 1940 he became Prime Minister and lead the country through World War II. He came back as PM in 1951. He was given state funeral and was voted greatest Briton by the public in 2002.

Alexander Fleming (1881-1955)
Born in Scotland and moved to London as a teenager. Trained as a doctor and researched influenza (the Flu). Famous for discovering penicillin in 1928. He won the Nobel prize for Medicine in 1945.

Clement Attlee (1883-1967)
Born in London, he studied in Oxford University to become a barrister. He became Labour MP and was Churchill deputy during the war. He formed a government in 1945 and oversaw nationalisation of major industries, the creation of the NHS, the implementation of a welfare system and improvement of workers conditions.

William Beveridge (1879-1963)
British economist who served as an MP as well. He is famous for his report in social insurance and allied services that provided the basis for the welfare system.

Richard Austen Butler (1902-1982)
Became conservative MP in 1923 and Minister for Education in 1941. He introduced free secondary education in England and Wales.

Dylan Thomas (1914-1953)
Welsh poet and writer most known for his play Under Milk Wood and the poem Do Not Go Gentle Into That Good Night

Mary Peters (1939-)
Born in Manchester and moved to Northern Ireland as a kid. Talented athlete she won an Olympic Gold Medal in Pentathlon in 1972. She raised money for athletics and became the women's British Olympic Team manager. She promotes sport in Northern Ireland and became a Dame of the British Empire in 2000.

Roald Dahl (1916-1990)
Welsh author. He served in the Royal Air force during World War II. Published many stories for kids including George's Marvellous medicine and Charlie and the Chocolate Factory.

Official style tests

This section provides you with 21 complete tests, for a total of 504 questions with their complete answer. Each of the tests follows the official Life in the UK exam format.

In the real exam, you will have 45 minutes to answer 24 questions about British history, traditions, and customs. You will be allowed to come back and review all previous questions so if you don't know an answer, don't spend too much time on it and move onto the next. I suggest you practice with a timer to make sure you can comfortably complete the test under 45 minutes.

Be very careful to read the question properly and fully. Even if you think you know the answer after reading a few words only. Sometimes a number or a word may be altered in the question.

Finally, remember that the test has two goals. Of course, primarily, the Life in the UK test is a mandatory part of your citizenship application. But it is also aimed at giving the future British citizen a base of knowledge about the country to which they are seeking to belong. These 21 tests below will help you with both. If, at times, an element of repetition appears between two questions, it is not a problem as it will help you remember the details better.

As much as you can, try to relax, get a glass of water, find a comfortable chair, ensure there is not too much noise or other distractions around you and get going. Good luck!

TEST 1

1. Which flag has a white cross on a blue background?

A. Scottish   C. Welsh
B. English   D. Irish

2. Where is the Cenotaph located?

A. Dorset   C. Whitehall
B. Trafalgar Square   D. Wiltshire

3. Who was Queen Elizabeth II married to?

A. Prince William   C. Prince Charles
B. Prince Philip   D. Prince Albert

4. Hanukkah is celebrated to remember the Jews' struggle for religious freedom. It is celebrated in November or December. How many nights and days does it last?

A. 6   C. 8
B. 7   D. 9

5. What happens to any driver who has either taken more than the acceptable quantity of alcohol or refuse to take the test?

A. Taken home   C. Given a warning
B. Arrested   D. Asked to provide medical certificate

6. In which century did Wales and England get united?

A. 12th Century   C. 14th Century
B. 13th Century   D. 15th Century

7. Which TWO records tell us about England during the time of William I?

A. Magna Carta
B. Canterbury Tales
C. Bayeux Tapestry
D. Domesday Book ✓

8. King Edward I of England annexed Wales to the crown of England by which statute?

A. Statute of Cardiff
B. Statute of Carmarthen
C. Statute of Gwynedd
D. Statute of Rhuddlan ✓

9. Which of the following statements is correct?

A. The first person to use the title Prime Minister was Sir Christopher Wren
B. The first person to use the title Prime Minister was Sir Robert Walpole

10. Who were the Jutes, Angles and Saxons?

A. Tribespeople from Northern Europe
B. Romans
C. Tribespeople from India
D. Tribespeople from Eastern Europe

11. Which TWO points about slavery are correct?

A. Slavery survived in the British Empire until the early 20th Century
B. Quakers set up the first anti-slavery groups
C. William Wilberforce was a leading abolitionist
D. The Royal Navy refused to stop ships carrying slaves

12. Which of the following statements is correct?

A. Police and Crime Commissioners (PCCs) are appointed by the local council.
B. Police and Crime Commissioners (PCCs) are appointed through a public election.

13. The 100 days before Easter are known as Lent. It is a time when Christians take time to reflect and prepare for Easter. Traditionally, people fast during this period.

A. True
B. False

14. Is the statement below TRUE or FALSE? The modern sport of Rugby originated in England in the early 19th century.

A.   True   B.   False

15. Who invented the Internet as we know it today? (World Wide Web)

A.   Peter Mansfield   C.   Clement Atlee
B.   Sir Tim Berners-Lee   D.   Wilfred Owen

16. Which country's national flower is a thistle?

A.   Wales   C.   Scotland
B.   England   D.   Northern Ireland

17. Who succeeded Margaret Thatcher as Prime Minister

A.   Kenneth Baker   C.   John Major
B.   Douglas Hurd   D.   Norman Tebbit

18. Is the following statement TRUE or FALSE? People over 75 can apply for a free TV licence, and blind people can get a 50% discount.

A.   True
B.   False

19. How old do you have to be to go into betting shops or gambling clubs?

A.   18   C.   16
B.   20   D.   21

20. What is an example of a Criminal Offence?

A.   Discrimination in the office   C.   Owing money
B.   Selling tobacco to under 18's   D.   Housing disputes

21. The Corn Laws were repealed in 1846. They prevented the import of cheap grain

A. True

B. False

22. Which of these is correct in the chronological order?

A. the Black Death, Canterbury Tales, Magna Carta

B. the Black Death, Magna Carta, Canterbury Tales

C. Canterbury Tales, the Black Death, Magna Carta

D. Magna Carta, the Black Death, Canterbury Tales

23. What did R. A. Butler introduce?

A. Free secondary education throughout England

B. Free college education in Scotland

C. Free university education in the UK

D. Free primary education in Wales

24. Who directed the two British films 'Brief Encounter' and 'Lawrence of Arabia'?

A. Hugh Hundson

B. Alfred Hitchcock

C. David Lean

D. William Walton

ANSWERS TO TEST 1

1. A. The national flag of Scotland consists of a white saltire defacing a blue field.

2. C. The Cenotaph is a monument located in Whitehall, the part of London that hosts most of UK Government's buildings. It is very close to Downing Street.

3. B. Queen Elizabeth was married to Prince Philip who passed away in April 2021

4. C. Hanukkah is observed for eight nights and days, starting on the 25th day of Kislev.

5. B. A driver under influence of alcohol beyond the acceptable dose or who refuse to take the test will be arrested.

6. D. In 1485, Henry Tudor seizes the throne and unites England and Wales under one Royal House.

7. C and D. William the Conqueror ruled between 1066 and 1087. The Bayeux Tapestry depicts events leading to William's conquest. The Domesday Book was created from the "Great Survey" of much of England and parts of Wales completed in 1086 by order of William.

8. D. The Statute of Rhuddlan provided the constitutional basis for the government of the Principality of Wales from 1284 until 1536.

9. B. Sir Robert Walpole became the first Prime minister in the 18th Century.

10. A. After the departure of the Romans, tribes from Northern Europe settled in Great Britain, among which the Jutes, the Angles and the Saxons.

11. B and C. the Quakers were first to establish anti-slavery committees in the 1780's and William Wilberforce brought the discussion on abolition to the parliament.

12. B. The public directly elect the Police and Crime Commissioners.

13. B. FALSE. Lent, the period before Easter commemorating Jesus fast in the desert lasts 40 days, not 100.

14. A. Rugby School football became popular throughout the UK in the 1850s, and 1860s.

15. B. In March 1989, Tim Berners-Lee proposed an information management system that would form the basis for the web.

16.C. The thistle has been the national emblem of Scotland since the reign of King Alexander III (1249–1286).

17. C. Sir John Major served as Prime Minister between 1990 and 1997.

18. A. True. People over 75 can apply for a free TV licence, and blind people can get a 50% discount.

19. A. You must be 18 to be allowed to bet or gamble.

20. B. It is a criminal offence to sell tobacco to those under the age of 18.

21. A. True. The Corn Laws were tariffs and other trade restrictions on imported food and corn enforced in the United Kingdom until 1846.

22. D. The correct order is Magna Carta (1215), the Black Death (1346-1353), Canterbury Tales (published circa 1400).

23. A. Richard Austen Butler was education minister between 1941 and 1945 in Churchill's cabinet. The Education Act of 1944 introduced many popular reforms, including free secondary education in England.

24. C. David Lean directed Brief Encounter (1945) and Lawrence of Arabia (1962)

TEST 2

1. The Glorious Revolution was called the "Glorious revolution" because there was no fighting in England and it guaranteed the power of Parliament

A.   True   B.   False

2. Which TWO are members of Parliament (MPs) responsible for?

A.   Representing every person in their   C.   Supporting the government on all
constituency   laws and decisions

B.   Representing the people who voted   D.   Commenting on and challenging
for them   what the government is doing.

3. How many members does the Scottish Parliament have?

A.   60   C.   129

B.   108   D.   320

4. At its peak the British Empire had an estimated population of just under 400 million.

A.   True   B.   False

5. There is no place in British society for which TWO of the following?

A.   Intolerance   C.   Democracy

B.   Extremism   D.   Politics

6. What special type of windows did many cathedrals built in the Middle Ages have?

A.   Stained glass   C.   Sash

B.   Mullioned   D.   Arched

7. As of today, who is the longest reigning British monarch?

A. Victoria

B. Henry VIII

C. Elizabeth II

D. Richard II

8. Which TWO of the following are British inventions?

A. Hovercraft

B. Golfcraft

C. Jet Engine

D. Helicopter

9. When did hereditary peers lose the automatic right to attend the House of Lords?

A. 1979

B. 1969

C. 1989

D. 1999

10. Mary Queen of Scots was related to Elizabeth I

A. True

B. False

11. In 1912, the British government promised Home Rule for Ireland. Which group within Ireland resisted the move with force?

A. The Catholics in the North

B. The Protestants in the North

C. The Protestants in the South

D. The Catholics in the South

12. Which of the following is a British invention or innovation?

A. Micro machines

B. A Turing machine

C. The telephone

D. The photocopier

13. People must meet which TWO conditions to be chosen for jury service?

A. Aged between 18 and 76

B. On the electoral register

C. Aged at least 50

D. A member of the police

14. There are 9 National Parks in the UK

A. True

B. False

15. What are the parliaments in Scotland, Wales and Northern Ireland also known as?

A. Formal institutions

B. Political parties

C. Devolved administrations

D. Local authorities

16. EU citizens who are resident in the UK can vote in national parliamentary elections.

A. Yes

B. Sometimes

C. No

17. Who was the monarch when the Book of Common Prayer was written to be used in the Church of England?

A. Edward VI

B. Henry VII

C. Henry VIII

D. Richard III

18. What percentage of the UK population lives in England?

A. 76%

B. 82%

C. 78%

D. 84%

19. Which of the options given below is not necessary for a new car?

A. Seat belts

B. Car insurance

C. MOT test

D. Road tax

20. What is not a fundamental principle of British life?

A. Driving a car

B. Looking after the environment

C. Looking after yourself and family

D. Treating others with fairness

21. Gertrude Jekyll was a famous garden designer.

A. True

B. False

22. The writer Roald Dahl served in the Royal Air Force during which conflict?

A. Second World War C. Korean War
B. The Suez Crisis D. First World War

23. Proceedings in Parliament cannot be reported in press or broadcast on television.

A. True B. False

24. Which country did Germany invade in 1939 that led to the UK declaring war on Germany?

A. Poland C. Austria
B. France D. Russia

ANSWERS TO TEST 2

1. A. True. The Glorious Revolution refers to the events of 1688–89 that saw King James II of England deposed and succeeded by one of his daughters and her husband.

2. A, D. Members of Parliament (MPs) represent everyone from their constituency and are responsible for commenting on or challenging the government.

3. C. the Scottish Parliament counts 129 seats.

4. A. True. The British Empire once counted a total population of nearly 400 million people.

5. A, B. Intolerance and extremism are not acceptable in British society.

6. A. Many cathedrals were built with stained glass windows, often depicting scenes and characters from the Bible.

7. C. Queen Elizabeth II reign started on February 6th, 1952. In February 2022, she has been reigning for 70 years. Victoria has the second longest reign of 63 years.

8. A, C. Christopher Cockerel was the first to demonstrate continued use of a hovercraft vehicle in the 1950's. Sir Frank Whittle is credited with developing a prototype of the jet engine in 1937.

9. D. The House of Lords Act 1999 removed the entitlement of most of the hereditary Peers to sit and vote in the House of Lords.

10. A. True. Mary Queen of Scots was first cousin once removed to Queen Elizabeth I of England. Her Grandmother was a sister of Henry VIII, Elizabeth's father.

11. B. In Ulster (Northern Ireland province), the Protestants opposed the Third Home Rule Bill of 1912.

12. B. Turing machines are hypothetical devices described by Alan Turing in 1936-37 that later would help develop modern computers. The concept was used by Turing during WWII to help break German's cypher.

13. A, B. Jury summons can be sent to anyone living in England as long as they are at least 18 and under 76 years of age and are registered voter.

14. B. False. The UK counts 15 National Parks: 10 in England, 3 in Wales and 2 in Scotland.

15. C. Parliaments in the other countries of the UK beside England are part of the devolved administrations.

16. C. No, even before Brexit, EU citizenship was not enough to grant national vote.

17. A. The original Book of Common prayer, published in 1549 during the reign of Edward VI, was a product of the English Reformation following the break with Rome.

18. D. England is the most populated part of the UK with c. 84% of UK population.

19. C. A new car doesn't need MOT. It becomes mandatory by the third anniversary of the car.

20. A. Driving a car is allowed to those holding a driving licence but it does not constitute of principle of British life.

21. A. True. Gertrude Jekyll (1843-1932), created over 400 gardens in the UK, Europe and America.

22. A. Roald Dahl served in the Royal Air Force (RAF) during the Second World War. He became a fighter pilot and, subsequently, an intelligence officer, rising to the rank of acting wing commander.

23. B. False. Parliament proceedings can be seen live.

24. A. Nazi Germany invaded Poland on September 1st, 1939, leading to the UK and France declaring war a couple days later.

TEST 3

1. Which of these UK landmarks is in Wales?

A.   Loch Lomond   C.   The Lake District

B.   The Giant's Causeway   D.   Snowdonia

2. British scientists were the first to clone which mammal successfully?

A.   Sheep   C.   Cat

B.   Cow   D.   Mouse

3. Which form of religion developed as a result of the Reformation?

A.   Protestantism   C.   Hinduism

B.   Methodism   D.   Baptism

4. When did King Edward I of England introduced the Statute of Rhuddlan by which Wales annexed to the Crown of England?

A.   1284   C.   1743

B.   1200   D.   1812

5. What is the correct name of the 2003 film directed by Kevin MacDonald?

A.   Touching the Top   C.   Touching the Void

B.   Touching the Untouchable   D.   Touching the Stone

6. Women were given the right to vote at the same age as men in 1982.

A.   True   B.   False

7. Which TWO are correct about Mary Stuart?

A. She was a week old when she became queen

B. She died during the Black Death

C. She was Elizabeth I's sister

D. She spent most of her childhood in France

8. What is the only major golf tournament held outside of the US?

A. Royal Ascot

B. The Open Championship

C. Wimbledon

D. The Premier League

9. Prior to 1832, constituencies with hardly any voters were called 'Pocket Boroughs'

A. True

B. False

10. Who was the skating partner of Christopher Dean when they won a gold medal in the 1984 Olympic Games?

A. Jayne Torvill

B. Mary Torvill

C. Mary Jayne

D. Katarina Jayne

11. Which of the following areas does civil law cover?

A. Burglary

B. Debt

C. Drunk and disorderly behaviour

D. Violent crime

12. In Scotland the national Church is the Church of Scotland. What kind of Church is it?

A. Presbyterian

B. Scientologist

C. Amish

D. Mormon

13. What did the Chartists campaign for?

A. The right to vote at 18

B. The right to vote for women

C. The right to vote for the workers

D. The right to vote at 21

14. Which Two British film actors have won Oscars?

A.   Tilda Swinton

B.   Colin firth

C.   Leonardo DiCaprio

D.   Jacky Stewart

15. Which event occurs each year on the third Sunday in June?

A.   Halloween

B.   Father's Day

C.   Mother's Day

D.   Easter Sunday

16. Which of the following statements is correct?

A.   The Wars of the Roses were between the Houses of Lancaster and York

B.   The Wars of the Roses were between the Houses of Windsor and Tudor

17. Is the statement below TRUE or FALSE? England, Scotland, Wales and Northern Ireland are governed only by the parliament sitting in Westminster.

A.   True

B.   False

18. In what English county can you see the hillfort at Maiden Castle?

A.   Cornwall

B.   Dorset

C.   East Lothian

D.   Danebury

19. How many Olympic gold medals has the Scottish cyclist, Sir Chris Hoy, won?

A.   7

B.   6

C.   2

D.   5

20. Rudyard Kipling was awarded which major prize in 1907?

A.   The Pulitzer prize

B.   The Somerset Maugham prize

C.   The Nobel prize

D.   The Man Booker prize

21. Which of the following statements is correct?

A.   After the election of a Conservative government in 1945, the NHS and a social security system was established.

B.   After the election of a Labour government in 1945, the NHS and a social security system was established

22. Where were the first farmers that came to Britain from?

A.   Northwest Europe

B.   Southwest Europe

C.   North Europe

D.   Southeast Europe

23. William Beveridge (later Lord Beveridge) was a British economist and social reformer. Which political party was he the leader of?

A.   The Conservative Party

B.   The Liberal Party

C.   The Labour Party

D.   The Green Party

24. Which TWO are Protestant Christian groups in the UK?

A.   Baptists

B.   Methodists

C.   Roman Catholics

D.   Hindus

ANSWERS TO TEST 3

1. D. Snowdonia is a mountainous region in north-western Wales and a national park of 823 square miles (2,130 km2) in area.

2. A. On July 5, 1996, Dolly the sheep—the first mammal to have been successfully cloned from an adult cell—is born at the Roslin Institute in Scotland.

3. A. The Protestant Reformation was a major movement within Western Christianity in 16th-century Europe that posed a religious and political challenge to the Catholic Church. It lead to the development of Protestantism.

4. A. The Statute of Rhuddlan provided the constitutional basis for the government of the Principality of Wales from 1284.

5. C. Touching the Void is a 2003 docudrama survival film directed by Kevin Macdonald.

6. B. False. The Equal Franchise Act gave women equal voting rights with men in 1928.

7. A, D. Mary was six days old when her father died, and she acceded to the throne. She lived in France between the ages of 5 and 18.

8. B. The Open Championship, often referred to as The Open or the British Open, is the oldest golf tournament in the world, founded in 1860.

9. A. True. Before the Reform Act 1832, a rotten or pocket borough was a parliamentary constituency with a very small electorate that could be used to gain influence.

10. A. Jayne Torvill and Christopher Dean's free program at the 1984 Winter Olympics in Sarajevo, performed to the music of Maurice Ravel's Bolero, received a total of twelve 6.0 marks, the highest possible score and the only time ever it was achieved.

11. B. Civil law is concerned with rights and property and deals with debts.

12. A. Church of Scotland, the national church in Scotland, accepted the Presbyterian faith during the 16th-century Reformation.

13. C. Chartism was a working-class movement, which emerged in 1836 and was most active between 1838 and 1848. They demanded right to vote for the working class.

14. A, B. In 2008, Tilda Swinton won the Oscar for Best Performance by an Actress in a Supporting Role for her performance as Karen Crowder in Michael Clayton.
In 2010, Colin Firth's portrayal of King George VI in Tom Hooper's The King's Speech won him an Oscar for Best Actor.

15. B. Father's Day is held on the third Sunday of June in the United Kingdom. It is a day to honour fathers and father figures.

16. A. The Wars of the Roses were a series of civil wars fought over control of the English throne in the mid-to-late fifteenth century. It was fought between supporters of two rival cadet branches of the royal House of Plantagenet: Lancaster and York.

17. B. False. The devolved nations, Scotland, Wales and Northern Ireland hold their own parliament and enjoy a certain level of self-government.

18. B. Maiden Castle in Dorset is one of the largest Iron Age hillforts in Europe

19. B. Sir Chris Hoy has won 6 Olympic Gold medals between 2004 and 2012.

20. C. The Nobel Prize in Literature 1907 was awarded to Rudyard Kipling.

21. B. in 1948, the Labour government created a National Health Service (NHS) as part of welfare reforms designed to guarantee basic levels of personal and social security

22. D. The culture of farming arrived in Britain some 6,000 years ago, likely brought by farmer from Southeast Europe, in particular around the Aegean sea.

23. B. In 1944, William Beveridge was elected a Liberal MP for Berwick-upon-Tweed. In 1945, he joined the House of Lords and became leader of the Liberal peers.

24. A, B. Baptists and Methodists are two Protestant Christian groups

TEST 4

1. After the Black Death, a new social class appeared, – owners of large areas of land. What were they called?

A. The Tudors   C. The Serfs
B. The Gentry   D. The Clans

2. Which TWO of these literary pieces are the work of Welsh poet Dylan Thomas, who lived from 1914 until his death in New York in 1953?

A. Brave New World   D. Do Not Go Gentle Into That Good
B. Under Milk Wood   Night
C. Nineteen Eighty-Four

3. What method is used to elect UK MPs?

A. Proportional Representation   C. Instant runoff
B. Popularity   D. First past the post system

4. What party won the election in 1945?

A. Conservative   C. Labour
B. Liberal Democrats   D. A coalition

5. Which country did NOT gain its independence from the British Empire in 1947?

A. India   C. Sri Lanka
B. Pakistan   D. The Caribbean

6. True or False. In England, police forces are independent of the government.

A. True   B. False

7. When did the American Colonies declare their independence?

A.   1776   C.   1749

B.   1733   D.   1783

8. Who discovered Insulin?

A.   John MacLeod   C.   Patrick Steptoe

B.   Mary Peters   D.   Ian Wilmot

9. Which ship was one of the first to sail around the world?

A.   Golden Hind   C.   The Ship of Royals

B.   HMS Victory   D.   Royal Yacht Britannia

10. Which charity works to preserve important buildings?

A.   NSPCC   C.   The Red Cross

B.   Age UK   D.   The National Trust

11. When is St David's day?

A.   17th of March   C.   1st of March

B.   23rd of April   D.   30th of November

12. Which of the following is the St Patron of Scotland:

A.   St David   C.   St George

B.   St Patrick   D.   St Andrew

13. Who was the first Briton to win the Olympic gold medal in the 10,000 meters?

A.   Bradley Wiggins   C.   Sir Chris Hoy

B.   Mo Farah   D.   David Weir

14. The European Convention on Human Rights is incorporated into UK law

A.   True   B.   False

15. What created the United Kingdom of Great Britain and Ireland?

A. The Great Union
B. The Acts of Union
C. The Act of the governments
D. The Great governments

16. Which of the following statements is correct?

A. County Courts deal with criminal cases
B. County Courts deal with civil disputes

17. Following the Bill of Rights, for which TWO are monarchs required to ask Parliament to renew funding for each year?

A. Army
B. Navy
C. Castles
D. Palaces

18. Where was Robert Burns from?

A. England
B. Northern Ireland
C. Wales
D. Scotland

19. Which British inventor was responsible for developing the television in the 1920s?

A. John Logie Baird
B. Sir Robert Watson-Watt
C. Sir Bernard Lovell
D. John Macleod

20. Where is the best-preserved prehistoric village "Skara Brae on Orkney" located?

A. England
B. Scotland
C. Wales
D. Ireland

21. Who was John Constable?

A. A landscape painter, most famous for his works of Dedham Vale
B. An important contributor to the 'pop art' movement of the 1960s
C. A Welsh artist, best known for his engravings and stained glass
D. A very successful Northern Irish portrait painter

22. Which flower is associated with England?

A. Rose
B. Daffodil
C. Thistle
D. Shamrock

23. Geoffrey Chaucer is associated with which of the following stories?

A. The London Tales
B. The Kent Tales
C. The Reading Tales
D. The Canterbury Tales

24. Who built the Tower of London?

A. Oliver Cromwell
B. Elizabeth I
C. Henry VIII
D. William the Conqueror

ANSWERS TO TEST 4

1. B. The Black Death killed many of the workers and drove many social changes. Skilled manpower was in huge demand and short supply leading some workers to earn enough to own land. The Gentry was born.

2. B, D. Dylan Thomas published Under Milk Wood in 1952 and Do Not Go Gentle Into That Good Night in 1951.

3. D. First Past The Post is a "plurality" voting system: the candidate who wins the most votes in each constituency is elected.

4. C. In 1945, the government led by Churchill was heavily defeated. The Labour Party, led by Attlee won a landslide victory and gained a majority of 145 seats.

5. D. The former British Caribbean islands achieved independence from 1962 to 1983.

6. A. True. Quite generally, English police forces are independent from the government. Outside London, publicly elected Police and Crime Commissioners (PCCs) are responsible for holding their police force to account and setting the direction of the force.

7. A. the independence of the American Colonies was signed in 1776, on July 4th.

8. A. John MacLeod received the 1923 Nobel prize in Physiology or Medicine for the discovery and isolation of insulin.

9. A. Golden Hind was a galleon captained by Francis Drake in his circumnavigation of the world between 1577 and 1580.

10. D. The National Trust protects and cares for places so people and nature can thrive.

11. C. Saint David's Day or the Feast of Saint David, is the feast day of Saint David, the patron saint of Wales, and falls on 1 March.

12. D. Saint Andrew is the patron saint of fishermen as well as Scotland and Russia.

13. B. At the London 2012 Olympics, Mo Farah won the 10,000 m gold.

14. A. True. The Human Rights Act 1998 sets out the fundamental rights and freedoms that everyone in the UK is entitled to. It incorporates the rights set out in the European Convention on Human Rights (ECHR) into domestic British law.

15. B. The Acts of Union 1800 were parallel acts of the Parliament of Great Britain and the Parliament of Ireland which united the Kingdom of Great Britain and the Kingdom of Ireland to create the United Kingdom of Great Britain and Ireland. The acts came into force on 1 January 1801.

16. B. The County Court is a court that deals with a variety of minor civil matters.

17. A, B. The English Bill of Rights was an act signed into law in 1689 by William III and Mary II. It imposes Parliamentary consent for the armed force (army, navy).

18. D. Robert Burns, was a Scottish poet and lyricist from the 18th century.

19. A. John Logie Baird was a Scottish inventor, electrical engineer, and innovator who demonstrated the world's first live working television system on 26 January 1926.

20. B. Skara Brae is a stone-built Neolithic settlement, located on the Bay of Skaill on the west coast of Mainland, the largest island in the Orkney archipelago of Scotland.

21. A. John Constable was an English landscape painter in the Romantic tradition from the 18th – 19th century.

22. A. The red rose is one of the three national symbols of England (alongside the St. George's cross and the Three Lions crest).

23. D. Geoffrey Chaucer was an English poet and author. Widely considered the greatest English poet of the Middle Ages, he is best known for The Canterbury Tales.

24. D. The tower was founded towards the end of 1066 as part of the Norman Conquest. The White Tower was built by William the Conqueror in 1078.

TEST 5

1. There are charities which may help people who cannot afford to pay a vet

A.   True   B.   False

2. What is the capital of Wales?

A.   Belfast   C.   Edinburgh

B.   Cardiff   D.   Swansea

3. The 'plantation' settlements in Ireland during the 17th century led to Catholic farmers replacing Protestant landowners.

A.   True   B.   False

4. Which of the following jobs is usually unpaid in England, Wales and Scotland?

A.   Wardens   C.   Civil lawyers

B.   Magistrates and Justices of the   D.   Policeman
Peace

5. What service does the TV licence pay for?

A.   Freeview channels   C.   Free radio and TV channels

B.   The BBC   D.   None of these

6. Dylan Thomas was a famous writer and poet from which country?

A.   England   C.   Wales

B.   Northern Ireland   D.   Scotland

7. The Prime Minister is the head of the Commonwealth

A.   True   B.   False

8. What Palace was a cast-iron and plate-glass building originally erected in Hyde Park, London, England, to house the Great Exhibition of 1851?

A.   Crystal Palace   C.   the Great Palace

B.   Gold Palace   D.   Dream Palace

9. It is legal to send a girl abroad for circumcision or cutting.

A.   True   B.   False

10. On St David's Day in Wales, which flower would you expect to see people wearing?

A.   Rose   C.   Daffodil

B.   Sunflower   D.   Poppy

11. Which of the following statements is correct?

A.   The civil service largely consists of political appointees

B.   The civil service is politically neutral

12. When is the public holiday, Boxing Day?

A.   The Sunday 2 weeks before Easter   C.   The day after New Year's day

B.   The Friday before Christmas   D.   The day after Christmas day

13. In the year 1588 the English defeated the Spanish Armada

A.   True   B.   False

14. Where can you get details about the small claims procedure?

A.   Your local polling station   C.   Any council

B.   Your local County Court   D.   The High Court

15. In which year did Margaret Thatcher became Member of Parliament?

A.   1949   C.   1979

B.   1959   D.   1989

16. In the 19th century, for which TWO of these materials the UK produced more than half the world production?

A.   Iron   C.   Potatoes

B.   Bronze   D.   Cotton Cloth

17. What is the name given to the 20th century conflict between those wishing for full Irish independence and those wishing to remain loyal to the UK government?

A.   The Troubles   C.   The Problems

B.   The Great Depression   D.   The Clearances

18. Which TWO of the following are major horse-racing events in the UK?

A.   Royal Ascot   C.   Champions League

B.   The Grand National   D.   Wimbledon

19. Which of the following statements is correct?

A.   Members of the public are not allowed to attend Youth Court hearings.

B.   Members of the public are allowed to attend Youth Court hearings.

20. Which organization looks after the Edinburgh Castle?

A.   The National Trust   C.   Historic Environment Scotland

B.   NSPCC   D.   The Red Cross

21. When did the Vikings first attack Britain?

A.   AD 798   C.   AD 879

B.   AD 789   D.   AD 897

22. Who captained the English football team in 1966?

A.   Sir Chris Hoy

B.   Bobby Moore

C.   Andy Murray

D.   Jackie Stewart

23. Where are the more serious civil cases dealt with in Scotland?

A.   Court of Session

B.   High Court

C.   Peace Courts

D.   Sheriff Court

24. Which of the following is a modern British architect?

A.   Dame Zaha Hadid

B.   Thomas Chippendale

C.   Dame Ellen MacArthur

D.   Sir William Golding

ANSWERS TO TEST 5

1. A. True. Several charities can provide pet owners some financial help with vet bills.

2. B. Cardiff is the capital and largest city of Wales, and the eleventh-largest in the United Kingdom.

3. B. False. During the 1680s and 90s, another major wave of settlement took place in Ireland. The new settlers were principally Scots. At this point Protestants and people of Scottish descent became an absolute majority of the population in Ulster. French Huguenots, who were Protestant, were also encouraged to settle in Ireland.

4. B. Magistrates (also called Justices of the Peace) are ordinary people who hear cases in court in their community. This is a volunteer role, but magistrates can claim expenses.

5. B. You must have a TV Licence if you watch or record BBC programmes on a TV, computer or other device as they're broadcast as well as if you download or watch BBC programmes on iPlayer – live, catch up or on demand.

6. C. Dylan Marlais Thomas was a Welsh poet and writer born in 1914. He died in 1953.

7. B. False. The Queen has been Head of the Commonwealth throughout her reign.

8. A. The Crystal Palace was a cast iron and plate glass structure, originally built in Hyde Park, London, to house the Great Exhibition of 1851.

9. B. False. Female genital mutilation (FGM) is illegal in the UK and considered child abuse, even if the girl is sent abroad for it.

10. C. The daffodil is Wales' national flower worn on St David's Day (1 March) in Wales.

11. B. A core value of the civil service is political impartiality. Civil servants serve the government, whatever its political persuasion.

12. D. Boxing Day is a holiday celebrated the day after Christmas Day, originally as a holiday to give gifts to the poor.

13. A. True. The Spanish Armada was a Habsburg Spanish fleet of 130 ships that sailed from Lisbon in late May 1588 to invade England. It was defeated by the British at the battle of Gravelines in August 1588.

14. B. You can contact the local County Court to help with small claims.

15. B. Margaret Thatcher won the Orpington seat and became an MP in 1959.

16. A, D. In the 19th century, the UK was leading the production of Iron and Cotton cloth.

17. A. The Troubles were an ethno-nationalist conflict in Northern Ireland that lasted about 30 years from the late 1960s to 1998.

18. A, B. Royal Ascot and the Grand National are UK major horse-racing events.

19. A. Youth courts are specially designed to make it easier for children to understand what is happening and feel less intimidated by their surroundings. Members of the public are excluded.

20. C. Historic Environment Scotland is a public body responsible for investigating, caring for and promoting Scotland's historic environment. It looks after Edinburgh Castle.

21. B. The earliest date given for a Viking raid is 789, when according to the Anglo-Saxon Chronicle, a group of Danes sailed to the Isle of Portland in Dorset.

22. B. Robert Frederick Chelsea Moore OBE and known as Bobbie Moore was an English professional footballer. He played for West Ham United and was the captain of the England national team that won the 1966 FIFA World Cup.

23. A. The Court of Session is the supreme civil court of Scotland. It sits in Parliament House in Edinburgh and is both a trial court and a court of appeal.

24. A. Dame Zaha Mohammad Hadid was a British Iraqi architect, artist and designer, recognised as a major figure in architecture of the late 20th and early 21st centuries.

TEST 6

1. Which TWO are British Overseas Territories?

A.   Ireland

B.   The Falkland Islands

C.   St Helena

D.   Hawaii

2. Who was Henry Purcell?

A.   A gardener

B.   An actor

C.   A composer

D.   A poet

3. What is known as Lent?

A.   The 40 days after Easter

B.   The 40 days before Easter

C.   The 40 days before Christmas

D.   The 40 days after Christmas

4. Which TWO of the following do lobby and pressure groups do?

A.   Influence government policy

B.   Represent views of businesses

C.   Organise protests

D.   Vote the laws

5. The British constitution is contained in a single written document.

A.   False

B.   True

6. The small claims procedure is a simple way for people to settle minor disputes.

A.   True

B.   False

7. Most shops in the UK open seven days a week.

A.   True

B.   False

8. For how many years did the Romans approximately stay in this country?

A. 400

B. 100

C. 200

D. 1000

9. Which TWO of the following are major outdoor music festivals?

A. Glastonbury

B. Isle of Wight Festival

C. Royal Ascot

D. The Grand National

10. What were TWO important aspects of the Reform Act of 1832?

A. It increases the number of people who could vote

B. It abolished slavery

C. It gave women the right to vote

D. It abolished rotten boroughs

11. The UK has a declining elderly population.

A. True

B. False

12. What were 'the Troubles' about?

A. Disagreement about Ireland becoming one country

B. Independence for Scotland

C. Reducing power over the monarch

D. Independence for Wales

13. Which TWO of the following must you have to pay tax on?

A. Shopping vouchers

B. Profits from self-employment

C. Family gifts

D. Revenue from dividends

14. Which TWO types of case can be held in County Courts?

A. Divorce

B. Trafficking

C. Murder

D. Breaches of contract

15. For UK citizens and permanent residents, what TWO freedoms are offered?

A. Free utility supply

B. Leaving work early on Friday

C. A right to a fair trial

D. Freedom of speech

16. In order to vote in elections what must you have done?

A. Have your name on the electoral register

B. Paid your income tax for the previous year

C. Registered with your local council

D. Pass an electoral test

17. Which is a monarch's ceremonial role?

A. Visiting abroad

B. Travelling through the UK

C. Opening a parliamentary session

D. Making policies

18. Where does the Prime Minister reside?

A. The Buckingham Palace

B. 76 Charlotte Street

C. 10 Downing Street

D. 1 Devonshire Terrace

19. What system automatically deducts tax from salary?

A. HMRC

B. PAYE

C. Self-Assessment

D. PAYG

20. What was the population of the UK in 1901?

A. 50 million

B. 40 million

C. 60 million

D. 27 million

21. What programme helps teenagers develop their skills?

A. The National Citizen Service

B. The Teenage Programme

C. The Youth Development Service

D. Youth Opportunities

22. What is the main role of the opposition in Parliament?

A.   To participate in public debates

B.   To represent the people of the UK

C.   To challenge the government

D.   To change laws

23. How often do you have to take a MOT test for an old vehicle?

A.   Every year

B.   Every 2 years

C.   Every 3 years

D.   Every 4 years

24. Where does the Scottish Grand National take place?

A.   Aintree

B.   Edinburgh

C.   Ayr

D.   Berkshire

ANSWERS TO TEST 6

1. B, C. The Falkland Islands and St Helena are part of the 14 British Overseas Territories.

2. C. Henry Purcell was an English composer from the 17th century.

3. B. Lent, in the Christian church, is a period of penitential preparation lasting 40 days before Easter.

4. A, B. Lobby groups represent the views of British businesses and try to influence government policy.

5. A. False. There is no written single British constitution.

6. A. True. A small claims procedure can help resolve minor dispute without having to go to court.

7. A. True. Shops in the UK can open 7 days a week.

8. A. Roman Britain is the period in classical antiquity when large parts of the island of Great Britain were under occupation by the Roman Empire. The occupation lasted from AD 43 to AD 410, so almost 400 years.

9. A, B. Two major music festivals are Glastonbury and the Isle of Wight Festival.

10. A, D. The Reform Act of 1832 increased the number of people eligible to vote and abolished the rotten boroughs.

11. B. False. The UK population is aging. The fastest increase in numbers is seen in those aged 85 and over.

12. A. The Troubles of the last half of the 20th Century centred on disagreements about a united Ireland.

13. B, D. You must be tax on dividends and self-employment profit.

14. A, D. County Courts will hear civil cases of divorce and contract breaches. Murder and trafficking are criminal cases.

15. C, D. Freedom of speech and a right to a fair trial are fundamentals rights offered to UK citizens.

16. A. You must be registered on the electoral register to be able to vote.

17. C. The Monarch opens the parliamentary session as part of their ceremonial role.

18. C. The Prime Minister's office and residence is located at 10 downing Street in London.

19. B. Tax on salary is deducted at source (before you get paid) by a system referred to as PAYE or Pay as You Earn.

20. B. in 1901, there were around 40 million people in the UK.

21. A. The National Citizen Service is a voluntary personal and social development programme for 16–17 year olds in England and Northern Ireland, funded largely by money from the UK Government.

22. C. In Parliament, the opposition challenges the government's decisions and policies.

23. A. After the car's third anniversary, an MOT is due annually.

24. C. The Scottish Grand National take place in Ayr, Ayrshire.

TEST 7

1. Who won the Tour de France?

A. Sir Chris Hoy
B. Bradley Wiggins
C. Mo Farah
D. Andy Murray

2. Who created James Bond?

A. Ian Fleming
B. JRR Tolkien
C. William Golding
D. J K Rowling

3. Which of these is not a valid bank note?

A. £5
B. £15
C. £20
D. £10

4. Which TWO new national bodies were established in 1999?

A. Welsh Assembly
B. Scottish Parliament
C. Irish Assembly
D. Northern Ireland Assembly

5. On the 5th of November what event is remembered each year?

A. Thanksgiving
B. The Queen's Birthday
C. Halloween
D. A plot by Guy Fawkes to blow up the Houses of Parliament

6. Which TWO of the following are Christian religious festivals that are celebrated in the UK?

A. Christmas
B. May Day
C. Halloween
D. Easter

7. The UK is governed by the parliament sitting in Westminster.

A.   False   B.   True

8. What government type was formed after the General Election in 2010?

A.   Two-party   C.   National

B.   Bi-party   D.   Coalition

9. Which of the following is the name of a novel by Jane Austen?

A.   Oliver Twist   C.   The Lord of the Flies

B.   Sense and Sensibility   D.   Great Expectations

10. Which of the following is a famous Stone Age site in the UK?

A.   Trafalgar Square   C.   Stonehenge

B.   Globe Theatre   D.   Buckingham Palace

11. Florence Nightingale (1820–1910) was famous for her work to improve the quality of nursing and hospital conditions.

A.   True   B.   False

12. Where is the National Assembly for Wales based?

A.   London   C.   Edinburgh

B.   Cardiff   D.   Newport

13. If you are learning to drive in the UK, you do not need to apply for a licence until you have passed the driving test.

A.   True   B.   False

14. During the English Civil War, which TWO were associated with King Charles I and Parliament?

A. Tories

B. Labour

C. Cavaliers

D. Roundheads

15. Which TWO are examples of civil law?

A. Housing disputes

B. Carrying firearms

C. Selling alcohol without a licence

D. Employment discrimination

16. In which county does the Eden Project stand in?

A. Berkshire

B. Cornwall

C. Devon

D. Hampshire

17. When were the last Welsh rebellion defeated?

A. 16th Century

B. 15th Century

C. 14th Century

D. 17th Century

18. When was the time of growing patriotism?

A. The Golden Age

B. The Iron Age

C. The Elizabethan period

D. The Victorian Age

19. How many national parks are there in the UK?

A. 15

B. 25

C. 10

D. 20

20. How are local councils funded?

A. Through local taxes and central government

B. From tax on local businesses

C. From local donations

D. From fundraising

21. Members of the public can be invited to join the jury in a youth court.

A.   True

B.   False

22. Which TWO are famous UK landmarks?

A.   Loch Lomond

B.   Lake Windermere

C.   Yellowstone Park

D.   Eiffel Tower

23. Who founded a monastery on the Island of Iona?

A.   St Patrick

B.   St David

C.   St Columba

D.   St Augustine

24. Which political party is still known as the Tories?

A.   Labour

B.   Conservative

C.   Liberal Democrats

D.   British National Party

ANSWERS TO TEST 7

1. B. Bradley Wiggins won the Tour de France in 2012.

2. A. Ian Lancaster Fleming was a British writer, journalist and naval intelligence officer who is best known for his James Bond series of spy novels.

3. B. There are no £15 bank notes.

4. A, B. In 1998, the UK Parliament passed three devolution Acts. Following this, the Scottish Parliament and the Welsh Assembly were set up in May 1999. The Northern Ireland Assembly first met on 1 July 1998.

5. D. Guy Fawkes was a member of a group of provincial English Catholics who were involved in the failed Gunpowder Plot of 1605. They had attempted to blow up the Houses of Parliament.

6. A, D. Christmas and Easter are Christian festivals celebrated in the UK.

7. A. False. The United Kingdom is a unitary state with devolution that is governed within the framework of a parliamentary democracy under a constitutional monarchy in which the monarch is the head of state while the Prime Minister of the United Kingdom is the head of government. The Parliament is there to represent the public's interests and make sure they are taken into account by the Government.

8. D. After the election of 2010, a coalition government was formed by the Conservatives and Liberal Democrats.

9. B. Jane Austen wrote Sense and Sensibility, published in 1811.

10. C. Stonehenge is a prehistoric monument on Salisbury Plain in Wiltshire, England.

11. A. True. Florence Nightingale was an English social reformer and the founder

of modern nursing. She came to prominence during the Crimean War, in which she organised care for wounded soldiers.

12. B. The Welsh Parliament is located in Cardiff.

13. B. False. You must apply for a provisional licence before taking lessons and the tests.

14. C, D. The English Civil War was a series of civil wars and political machinations between Parliamentarians (Roundheads) and Royalists (Cavaliers), mainly over the manner of England's governance and issues of religious freedom.

15. A, D. Housing disputes and employment discrimination are matters of civil law.

16. B. The Eden Project is a visitor attraction in Cornwall, England, UK

17. B. The Welsh Revolt or Last War of Independence was an uprising of the Welsh between 1400 and 1415 against the Kingdom of England. It was the last major manifestation of a Welsh independence movement before the incorporation of Wales into England.

18. C. The Elizabethan period (1558-1603) saw an increase in patriotism. It is often called the golden age of British history.

19. A. there are 15 national parks in the UK.

20. A. Local councils get their money from government and by raising local taxes.

21. B. False. There is no jury in youth court.

22. A, B. Loch Lomond and Lake Windermere are British landmarks.

23. C. Iona is a small island in the Inner Hebrides. It has been described as the birthplace of Christianity in Scotland. St Columba and 12 companions arrived from Ireland in AD 563.

24. B. The Conservative Party, officially the Conservative and Unionist Party, is also known colloquially as the Tories.

TEST 8

1. Who developed ideas about economics during the enlightenment which are still referred to today?

A. James Watt

B. David Hume

C. Adam Smith

D. Isaac Newton

2. One TV licence covers all of the equipment at one address, but people who rent different rooms in a shared house must buy a separate TV licence

A. True

B. False

3. What group of refugees came to settle in England between 1680 and 1720?

A. Scottish

B. Indians

C. Scandinavian

D. Huguenots

4. Ted Hughes and John Masefield are both famous as what?

A. Actors

B. Poets

C. Dancers

D. Fighters

5. Which TWO major welfare changes were introduced between 1945 and 1950?

A. The NHS

B. A social security system for everyone

C. Employments benefits

D. State pension

6. EastEnders and Coronation Street are popular TV shows

A. True

B. False

7. The Scottish Parliament may pass laws on

A.   Foreign affairs   C.   The army

B.   General economic policy   D.   Education

8. Which of these countries was part of the British Empire during Victoria's reign?

A.   France   C.   India

B.   USA   D.   Germany

9. What happened in 1928 to make it an important date in the history of women's rights?

A.   Wives were given the right to keep   C.   Women were made legally
their own earnings   responsible for their children's crime

B.   Women were given the right to vote   D.   Equal pay laws were passed

10. Which famous British novelist wrote Brighton Rock?

A.   William Golding   C.   Graham Greene

B.   Arthur Conan Doyle   D.   William Worstworth

11. Civil Servants are accountable to

A.   Members of Parliament   C.   The national party

B.   Ministers   D.   the Queen

12. Which of these birds is traditionally associated with Christmas in the UK?

A.   Chicken   C.   Turkey

B.   Swan   D.   Pigeon

13. English kings fought a long war with France which was known as

A.   The English War   C.   The French War

B.   The Ten Year War   D.   The Hundred Year War

14. Who invaded the Falkland Islands in 1982?

A. Spain   C. Portugal

B. Argentina   D. Columbia

15. After drivers reach 70 years old, their driving licence is valid for how many years?

A. 1   C. 3

B. 2   D. 4

16. The Scottish Parliament building opened in 2004.

A. True   B. False

17. Where did Charles II hide to escape from Cromwell's army?

A. In a house attic   C. In an oak tree

B. In a church   D. In a garden

18. Whose approval Henry VIII needed to divorce his first wife?

A. The Archbishop of Canterbury   C. Parliament

B. The king of France   D. The Pope

19. The UK belongs to which TWO international bodies?

A. The North Atlantic Free Trade Agreement (NAFTA)   C. The Commonwealth

B. The North Atlantic Treaty Organization (NATO)   D. Collective Security Treaty Organization (CSTO)

20. What medal was introduced during the Crimean War?

A. The Medal of Honour   C. Elizabeth gold

B. The Victoria Cross   D. The Elizabeth Medal

21. Which charity is working with older people?

A.   Age UK
B.   NSPCC

C.   The Red Cross
D.   National Trust

22. William III of England, Wales and Ireland was which king of Scotland?

A.   William IV
B.   William II

C.   William I
D.   William III

23. Which of the following is a document or piece of legislation that sets out fundamental rights or freedoms?

A.   The Habeas Corpus Act
B.   The UK Constitution

C.   the Act of Union
D.   The Statute of Rhuddlan

24. What was encouraged to develop the UK economy in 1950?

A.   Education
B.   Slave Trade

C.   Immigration
D.   Savings Accounts

ANSWERS TO TEST 8

1. C. Adam Smith was an 18th century Scottish economist, a pioneer of political economy and key figure during the Scottish Enlightenment.

2. A. True. A TV licence covers all equipment at the same address but for one family only.

3. D. Huguenots were French Protestants. Persecuted by the French Catholic government in the 17th century, many fled the country and found refuge in England.

4. B. Edward James Hughes and John Masefield were 20th century English poets and writers.

5. A, B. Both the NHS and universal social security were introduced by the Labour government between 1945 and 1950.

6. A. True. EastEnders and Coronation street are fictional TV series following the life of ordinary people.

7. D. The Scottish Parliament can pass legislation on devolved matters including education, health, agriculture, and justice.

8. C. Queen Victoria was also Empress of India.

9. B. 1928: The Representation of the People Act 1928 gave women in England, Wales and Scotland the vote on the same terms as men.

10. C. Henry Graham Greene was an English writer and journalist regarded by many as one of the leading English novelists of the 20th century.

11. B. Civil servants respond to the ministers they serve.

12. C. The Christmas turkey tradition can be traced back to Henry VIII, who decided to

make the bird a staple for the festive day.

13. D. The Hundred Years' War was a series of armed conflicts between the kingdoms of England and France during the Late Middle Ages.

14. B. Argentina invade the Falkland Islands in 1982, thus triggering the 10 week Falklands War.

15. C. Once you reach 70, you must renew your driving licence every 3 years

16. A. True. Members of the Scottish Parliament held their first debate in the new building on 7 September 2004

17. C. The future King Charles II of England hid in an oak tree to escape the Roundheads following the Battle of Worcester in 1651.

18. D. Henry VIII wanted to divorce his first wife, Catherine of Aragon, but needed the Pope's approval first.

19. B, C. The UK is a member of NATO and the Commonwealth.

20. B. In 1856, Queen Victoria instructed the War Office to strike a new medal to recognise acts of valour during the Crimean War. It would become known as the Victoria Cross.

21. A. Age UK is the leading UK charity helping older people.

22. B. William III, also known as William of Orange was William II of Scotland.

23. A. The Habeas Corpus Act 1679 is an Act of Parliament in England during the reign of King Charles II. It guarantees the right to a fair trial.

24. C. Immigration in 1950's was used to boost the economy.

TEST 9

1. Which TWO are required for people to be randomly selected for jury service?

A. Aged at least 16

B. Aged between 18 and 70

C. Be on the electoral register

D. Be on the jury register

2. Why did the Roman Emperor Hadrian build a wall across parts of northern England?

A. To form settlements

B. To keep out the Picts

C. To keep out the Normans

D. To prevent theft of his livestock

3. The Welsh Parliament is also called

A. Holyrood

B. Senedd

C. Westminster

D. Dáil Éireann

4. Who designed New Delhi to be the seat of government in India?

A. Sir Edwin Lutyens

B. Sir Christopher Wren

C. Inigo jones

D. Robert Adam

5. When did William of Orange invade England?

A. 1692

B. 1688

C. 1684

D. 1696

6. Which of the following is a famous British film?

A. Passport to Paddington

B. Passport to Pimlico

C. Passport to Panama

D. Passport to Portsmouth

7. When did the Battle of Agincourt take place?

A.   1200

B.   1613

C.   1415

D.   1716

8. Who did Henry VII marry to form an alliance

A.   Elizabeth Tudor

B.   Elizabeth of York

C.   Elizabeth of Lancaster

D.   Catherine of Aragon

9. When did Queen Elizabeth II celebrate her Diamond Jubilee?

A.   2011

B.   2012

C.   2013

D.   2014

10. What is Diwali popularly known as?

A.   The Festival of Fireworks

B.   The Festival of Darkness

C.   The Festival of Lights

D.   The Festival of Colours

11. What was the name of the plague that killed a third of English population in 1348?

A.   The White Death

B.   The Pig Flu

C.   The Bird Flu

D.   The Black Death

12. When was The National Trust founded?

A.   1945

B.   1789

C.   1895

D.   1845

13. Where can you find a solicitor in the UK?

A.   The Citizen Advice Bureau

B.   A police station

C.   In a Youth Court

D.   In a law firm

14. Mothering Sunday is two weeks before Easter

A.   False

B.   True

176

15. Which of these is NOT a city in the UK?

A.   Leeds   C.   Bradford
B.   Brussels   D.   Blackpool

16. Do magistrates need legal qualifications?

A.   Yes   B.   No

17. Which play was written by Shakespeare

A.   Hamlet   C.   Freedom of Love
B.   Before the Dawn   D.   Come, walk with me

18. What is Yorkshire pudding?

A.   Batter cooked in the oven   C.   A pastry filled with meet and potato
B.   A dessert of raisins and dates D.   Bacon, Eggs and sausage

19. What was an important English export in the Middle Ages?

A.   Glass   C.   Potatoes
B.   Wool   D.   Stone

20. Who is the fastest person to have sailed around the world, single-handed?

A.   Dame Mary Peters   C.   Dame Agatha Christie
B.   Dame Ellen MacArthur   D.   Dame Kelly Holmes

21. Women received the right to vote at the same age as men in which year?

A.   1918   C.   1938
B.   1928   D.   1948

22. Where was the Battle of Britain fought?

A.   Air   C.   Sea
B.   Land   D.   Underground

23. Which industry has an annual event that gives out Brit awards?

A.   Radio

B.   Film

C.   Sport

D.   Music

24. If you watch TV without a licence, you will receive a fine of up to

A.   £200

B.   £400

C.   £500

D.   £1000

ANSWERS TO TEST 9

1. B, C. People between the age of 18 and 70 and registered to vote can be called for jury service.

2. B. Hadrian's Wall is a former defensive fortification of the Roman province of Britannia, begun in AD 122 in the reign of the emperor Hadrian to separate Romans from the barbarians to the north including the Picts.

3. B. The Senedd is officially known as Senedd Cymru in Welsh and the Welsh Parliament in English.

4. A. sir Edwin Lutyens was an English architect born in 1869. He played an instrumental role in designing and building New Delhi, which would later on serve as the seat of the Government of India.

5. B. In response to an invitation of seven peers (the so-called Immortal Seven) to invade England in order to preserve Protestantism, the Dutch ruler William of Orange landed at Brixham with an invasion force on 5 November 1688.

6. B. Passport to Pimlico is a 1949 British comedy film.

7. C. The Battle of Agincourt was an English victory in the Hundred Years' War. It took place on 25 October 1415 near Azincourt, in northern France.

8. B. Elizabeth of York married Henry VII in 1486. As they were from rival houses, their union crystalised the end of the war of roses.

9. B. Queen Elizabeth II celebrate her Diamond Jubilee (60 years reign) in 2012.

10. C. Diwali is a Festival of Lights and one of the major festivals celebrated by Hindus, Jains, and Sikhs.

11. D. The Black Death was a bubonic plague pandemic between 1346 to 1353.

12. C. The National Trust for Places of Historic Interest or Natural Beauty is a charity and membership organisation for heritage conservation in England, Wales and Northern Ireland. It was founded in 1895.

13. A. Citizens Advice Bureau is an independent organisation specialising in confidential information and advice to assist people with legal, debt, consumer, housing, and other problems in the United Kingdom.

14. A. False. Mothering Sunday is a day honouring mothers celebrated in the United Kingdom and Ireland on the fourth Sunday in Lent.

15. B. Brussels is the capital of Belgium.

16. B. No. Magistrates are volunteers who hear cases in courts in their community. They don't require qualifications but can receive training.

17. A. Hamlet was written by Shakespeare.

18. A. A Yorkshire pudding is a baked pudding made from a batter of eggs, flour, and milk or water.

19. C. England exported a lot of potatoes during the Middle Ages.

20. B. Dame Ellen Patricia MacArthur is a successful solo long-distance yachtswoman. In 2005, she sailed around the world in just over 71 days.

21. B. Women could vote like men did from 1928.

22. A. The Battle of Britain, also known as the Air Battle for England, was a military campaign of the Second World War against large-scale air raids by Nazi Germany's air force, the Luftwaffe.

23. D. The BRIT Awards are the British Phonographic Industry's annual music awards.

24. D. The fine for watching TV without a licence can reach £1000.

TEST 10

1. What nationality is Sir Robert Watson-Watt, who developed radar in the 1930s?

A.   English

B.   Scottish

C.   Welsh

D.   Irish

2. The day before Lent starts is called

A.   Boxing Day

B.   Good Friday

C.   Shrove Tuesday

D.   April Fool's Day

3. Ministers form the Cabinet, a committee which meets every:

A.   Day

B.   Week

C.   Fortnight

D.   Month

4. Who introduce shampoo in England?

A.   Sir Tim Berners-Lee

B.   Clement Atlee

C.   Sake Dean Mahomet

D.   Samuel Crompton

5.The Book of Common Prayer introduced by Edward VI was in which language?

A.   Welsh

B.   Engllsh

C.   Latin

D.   Gaelic

6. D-Day is when the British evacuated French troops from Normandy during WWII.

A.   False

B.   True

7.The Scottish Parliament was formed in 1998 and sits in Edinburgh

A.　　False

B.　　True

8. Rugby is the name of an English town.

A.　　True

B.　　False

9. Devolved administrations in the UK have power other which?

A.　　Education

B.　　Defence

C.　　Immigration

D.　　Foreign Affair

10. The Wars of the Roses saw wars between rival branches of which Royal House?

A.　　House of Wessex

B.　　House of York

C.　　House of Plantagenet

D.　　House of Lancaster

11. When did the Romans leave Britain?

A.　　2nd century

B.　　3rd century

C.　　4th century

D.　　5th century

12. When is Bonfire night celebrated?

A.　　April 1st

B.　　May 29th

C.　　November 5th

D.　　December 25th

13. The first people lived in Britain during which period?

A.　　The Steel Age

B.　　The bronze Age

C.　　The Rock Age

D.　　The Stone Age

14. What's the age requirement to drink wine with a meal when accompanied with someone over 18?

A.　　16

B.　　17

C.　　18

D.　　21

15. Catherine of Aragon, wife of Henry VIII was a princess from which country?

A.   England

B.   Spain

C.   France

D.   Wales

16. Who became the first Archbishop of Canterbury?

A.   St Columba

B.   St George

C.   St Augustine

D.   St Patrick

17. When is Halloween celebrated?

A.   31 October

B.   30 November

C.   30 October

D.   31 November

18. Where is the Royal Crescent located?

A.   London

B.   Bath

C.   Cardiff

D.   Edinburgh

19. How long does Diwali normally last for?

A.   5 days

B.   8 days

C.   7 days

D.   10 days

20. Who are TWO famous Paralympians?

A.   Dame Ellen MacArthur

B.   Ellie Simmonds

C.   Baroness Tanni Grey-Thompson

D.   Jessica Ennis

21. The Speaker of the House of Commons is chosen by

A.   The Prime Minister

B.   By the monarch

C.   By the public

D.   Through an election by their peers.

22. Bishops of the Church of England are allowed to sit in the House of Lords.

A.   True

B.   False

23. After the abolition of slavery in 1833, migrants came from which country to replace slaves?

A.   Australia

B.   France

C.   China

D.   Russia

24. What is the Giant's Causeway made of?

A.   Stone

B.   Bronze

C.   Marble

D.   Volcanic Lava

ANSWERS TO TEST 10

1. B. Sir Robert Watson-Watt was a Scottish pioneer of radio direction finding and radar technology.

2.C. Shrove Tuesday is the day before Ash Wednesday, observed in many Christian countries as the start of Lent. Pancakes are traditionally eaten on Shrove Tuesday.

3. B. the Cabinet meets weekly

4. C. Sake Dean Mahomed was an Indian surgeon and entrepreneur. He introduced shampoo baths to Europe, where he offered therapeutic massage.

5. B. The Book of Common Prayer of 1549 was the first prayer book to include the complete forms of service for daily and Sunday worship in English.

6. A. False. D-Day was the Allied forces invasion of Normandy in June 1944.

7. A. False. The Scottish Parliament was created in 1999, not 1998.

8. A. True. Rugby is a market town in eastern Warwickshire, England, close to the River Avon.

9. A. Devolved administrations can pass legislation on matters of education.

10. C. The Wars of the Roses were fought between supporters of two rival cadet branches of the royal House of Plantagenet.

11. D. The traditional view of historians is of a widespread economic decline at the beginning of the 5th century. Traces of the Romans in England after 410 are very scarce.

12. C. Bonfire Night and Fireworks Night, is an annual commemoration observed on 5 November.

13. D. first settlements in Britain go back to the Stone Age. Over 6000 years ago.

14. A. If accompanied by an adult, a 16 year old is allowed wine with their meal.

15. B. Catherine of Aragon was born in Castille, in today's Spain.

16. C. Augustine of Canterbury was a monk who became the first Archbishop of Canterbury in the year 597.

17. A. Halloween is a celebration observed in many countries on 31 October.

18. B. The Royal Crescent is a row of 30 terraced houses laid out in a sweeping crescent in the city of Bath, England.

19. A. The Diwali Festival usually lasts five days.

20. B, C. Eleanor May Simmonds is a British former Paralympian swimmer who won two gold medals in the 2008 Summer Paralympics in Beijing. Baroness Tanni Grey-Thompson was a wheelchair racer. During her Paralympic career, she won 16 medals.

21. D. MPs elect the Speaker of the House of commons from amongst their own ranks.

22. A. True. the Lords Spiritual is composed of Church of England archbishops and bishops.

23. C. Slaves were often replaced by Chinese migrants after the abolition of slavery.

24. D. The Giant's Causeway, in Northern Ireland, is an area of about 40,000 interlocking basalt columns, the result of an ancient volcanic fissure eruption.

TEST 11

1. Which of the following is a fundamental principle of British life?

A. Communism

B. Intolerance

C. Individual liberty

D. Inequity

2. Who created the character Sherlock Holmes?

A. Evelyn Waugh

B. Sir Kingsley Amis

C. Graham Greene

D. Sir Arthur Conan Doyle

3. Who was the leader of the suffragettes, the group that campaigned for women's rights to vote?

A. Queen Victoria

B. Oliver Cromwell

C. Florence Nightingale

D. Emmeline Pankhurst

4. What medal did Mary Peters win in the 1972 Olympics?

A. She did not win any medals

B. Silver

C. Gold

D. Bronze

5. What was the religion of the Puritans?

A. Hindu

B. Catholic

C. Sikh

D. Protestant

6. When did the Emancipation Act abolish slavery throughout the British Empire?

A. 1835

B. 1823

C. 1807

D. 1833

7. What was achieved with the Magna Carta?

A. It restricted the King's power

B. It increased the King's power

C. It restricted farmers' rights

D. It increased women's power

8. What is the judiciary responsible for?

A. Interpreting the law

B. Deciding whether a person is guilty

C. Putting people in prison

D. D. Looking after a jury

9. What gave rise to the Dunkirk spirit?

A. When the German air force bombed London and other cities at night-time

B. The evacuation of Allied soldiers from France during World War II

C. When new social classes appeared after the Black Death

D. The period when many refugees called Huguenots came from France

10. Which of the following statements is true?

A. Women in Britain today make up about half of the workforce.

B. Women in Britain today make up about one quarter of the workforce.

11. What type of literature are the Canterbury Tales?

A. Poems

B. Novels

C. Jokes

D. Fables

12. What charity works to preserve important UK buildings, coastline and countryside?

A. Shelter

B. Age UK

C. Crisis

D. The National Trust

13. Which two houses form the UK Parliament?

A. The House of Lords

B. House of Members

C. House of Commons

D. House of Fraser

14. How many member states does the Commonwealth have?

A. 5

B. 27

C. 38

D. 54

15. When is Hogmanay celebrated?

A. 25th of December

B. 2nd of January

C. 1st of January

D. 31st of December

16. Who was the tribal leader who fought against the Romans?

A. Columba

B. Claudius

C. Hadrian

D. Boudica

17. Why were canals built during the Industrial Revolution?

A. To link the factories to towns and cities and to the ports

B. To make space for the large fleet of British ships

C. To increase the number of water mills in the UK

D. To increase the amount of water in towns and cities

18. Which of the following is a rugby competition?

A. The Scottish Grand National

B. The Wimbledon Championships

C. The Ashes

D. The Six Nations Championship

19. Where do Beefeaters serve as tour guides?

A. The Houses of the Parliament

B. The Tower of London

C. The O2

D. The Big Ben

20. Who is the spiritual leader of the Church of England?

A. The Archbishop of Canterbury

B. The Archbishop of London

C. The Archbishop of Birmingham

D. The Archbishop of Manchester

21. Who defeated the Vikings?

A. Harold

B. Edward I of England

C. King Arthur

D. King Alfred the Great

22. In the UK, you have to be 21 years old to be able to vote in a general election.

A. True

B. False

23. What was Edward Elgar famous for?

A. He was a musician

B. He was a tennis player

C. He was a comedian

D. He was an actor

24. What was Isaac Newton known for?

A. Insulin

B. Gravity

C. Penicillin

D. Steam power

ANSWERS TO TEST 11

1. C. Individual liberty is a fundamental principle of British Life.

2. D. Sir Arthur Conan Doyle was a British writer and physician. He created the character Sherlock Holmes in 1887 for A Study in Scarlet.

3. D. Emmeline Pankhurst was an English political activist best remembered for organising the UK suffragette movement and helping women win the right to vote.

4. C. Lady Mary Elizabeth Peters is a Northern Irish former athlete. She won gold for the Pentathlon at the 1972 Olympics.

5. D. The Puritans were English Protestants during the 16th and 17th centuries.

6. D. In August 1833, the Slave Emancipation Act was passed, giving all slaves in the British empire their freedom.

7. A. Magna Carta is a royal charter of rights agreed to by King John of England on 15 June 1215. It restricted the King's power.

8. A. The judiciary is that branch of the government that interprets the law, settles disputes and administers justice to all citizens.

9. B. The Dunkirk spirit was born from the evacuation of British and Allied soldiers from the French harbour of Dunkirk in 1940. It demonstrates an attitude of being very strong in a difficult situation and refusing to accept defeat.

10. A. Around half of workers in Britain today are women.

11. A. The tales of Canterbury is a collection of 24 poems written in verse.

12. D. Preservation and conservation are two main objectives of The National Trust.

13. A, C. The UK Parliament has two Houses that work on behalf of UK citizens: The House of Lords and the House of Commons.

14. D. The Commonwealth is a political association of 54 member states, almost all of which are former territories of the British Empire.

15. D. Hogmanay is the Scots word for the last day of the year and is synonymous with the celebration of the New Year in the Scottish manner. It is celebrated on 31 December.

16. D. Boudica, also known as Boadicea, was a queen of the British Iceni tribe who led an uprising against the conquering forces of the Roman Empire in AD 60 or 61.

17. A. Canals were built to create links between factories, towns, and harbours.

18. D. The Six Nations Championship is an annual international men's rugby union competition.

19. B. The Beefeaters are the ceremonial guardians of the Tower of London.

20. A. The Archbishop of Canterbury is the senior bishop and principal leader of the Church of England.

21. D. At the battle of Ashdown in 871, King Alfred the Great routed the Viking army in a fiercely fought uphill assault.

22. B. False. To vote in a general election you must be 18 or over on the day of the election.

23. A. Sir Edward William Elgar was an English composer born in 1857.

24. B. Sir Isaac Newton was an English mathematician, physicist, astronomer, theologian, and author widely recognised as one of the most influential scientists. He came up with his gravitational theory in 1665.

TEST 12

1. Who is the patron Saint of England?

A. St George

B. St Patrick

C. St David

D. St Andrew

2. Why were women given the right to vote?

A. In recognition of the contribution women made to the war effort during the First World War

B. In recognition of the contribution women made to the war effort during the Second World War

C. In recognition of the contribution women made to the war effort during the Crimean War

D. In recognition of the contribution women made to the war effort during the Civil War

3. Which two universities participate in an annual rowing race that takes place on the River Thames?

A. The University of Oxford

B. The University of Cambridge

C. The University of Manchester

D. The University of Warwick

4. Which sport can be traced back to the 15th century in Scotland?

A. Golf

B. Tennis

C. Football

D. Rugby

5. How many members does a jury have in England and Wales?

A. 9

B. 12

C. 15

D. 20

6. What did the Scottish John Logie Baird develop?

A. Television

B. Radar

C. Personal computer

D. Radio

7. What should you do to make a complaint about the police (choose two answers)?

A. Write a complaint letter to the House of Commons

B. Go to the Police station directly

C. Write to the Chief Constable of the police force involved

D. Write to your MP

8. Who did Britain fight against in the Crimean War?

A. Turkey

B. Russia

C. France

D. Germany

9. Which two languages combined to become one English language?

A. Latin

B. Anglo-Saxon

C. Proto-Celtic

D. Norman French

10. What is the name of the holiday when banks and many other businesses are closed for the day?

A. Credit Holidays

B. Branch Holidays

C. Bank Holidays

D. Business Holidays

11. Who built a wall in the north of England to keep out the Picts (ancestors of the Scottish people)?

A. Boudicca

B. Emperor Hadrian

C. Emperor Claudius

D. Julius Caesar

12. How many members does the Welsh Assembly have?

A. 150

B. 120

C. 90

D. 60

194

13. *Where does "the Fringe" festival take place?*

A.   Fraserburgh   C.   Inverness
B.   Edinburgh   D.   St Andrews

14. *During the reign of Elizabeth I, a large fleet of ships was sent to England to conquer the country and to restore Catholicism, where did this fleet come from?*

A.   France   C.   Spain
B.   Portugal   D.   Italy

15. *In 1348, a disease, probably a form of plague, came to Britain. What was it called?*

A.   Malaria   C.   Black Death
B.   White Death   D.   Giant Evil

16. *The Victoria Cross medal was introduced during which war?*

A.   The Hundred Years War   C.   The Crimean War
B.   The First World War   D.   The Second World War

17. *What percentage of the total UK population lives in Wales?*

A.   5%   C.   1%
B.   3%   D.   8%

18. *When did English become the official language for documents?*

A.   1400
B.   1451
C.   1554
D.   1502

19. *Which TWO are famous British fashion designers?*

A.   Robert Adam   C.   Isambard Kingdom Brunel
B.   Mary Quant   D.   Alexander McQueen

20. During the civil war of 1455, what colour rose was the symbol of the House of Lancaster?

A.   Red   C.   Red and White
B.   White   D.   Orange

21. George and Robert Stephenson were famous pioneers of which industry?

A.   Railway engines   C.   Agricultural
B.   Canal building   D.   Automobile

22. St Augustine led missionaries from Rome. When did he spread Christianity?

A.   In the 3rd century AD   C.   In the 6th century AD
B.   In the 4th century AD   D.   In the 8th century AD

23. When did motor-car racing start in the UK?

A.   1899   C.   1902
B.   1896   D.   1930s

24. During the reigns of Elizabeth I and James I, the English government encouraged Scottish and English Protestants to settle in which Irish province?

A.   Pale   C.   Grimsby
B.   Ulster   D.   Dublin

ANSWERS TO TEST 12

1. A. St George is the patron saint of England.

2. A. In recognition of their contribution during the first World War, women over the age of 30 who met a property qualification were granted vote.

3. A, B. The annual Oxford-Cambridge University Boat Race was first raced in 1829.

4. A. The modern game of golf originated in 15th-century Scotland,

5. B. A jury of 12 people decide the outcome of a criminal trial in England and Wales.

6. A. Scottish inventor John Logie Baird developed the television in the early 1920's.

7. B, C. Members of the public can complain about the police by going to the police station or writing to the Chief Constable of the force involved.

8. B. The Crimean War was a military conflict fought from October 1853 to February 1856 in an alliance of France, the Ottoman Empire, the United Kingdom and Sardinia won against Russia.

9. B, C. English originated from Proto-Celtic languages and from Anglo-Saxon languages brought to Britain in the mid 5th to 7th centuries AD by Anglo-Saxon migrants from what is now northwest Germany, southern Denmark and the Netherlands.

10. C. A bank holiday is a public holiday when banks and many other businesses are closed for the day.

11. B. Roman emperor Hadrian built the wall that bears his name to protect against barbarian from the North.

12. D. The Welsh Assembly has 60 seats.

13. B. The Fringe is an arts festival that presents a variety of plays, performances, and exhibitions every August in Edinburgh.

14. C. The fleet came from Spain and was called the Spanish Armada.

15. C. The Black Death was a bubonic plague pandemic occurring in Afro-Eurasia in the 14th century.

16. C. The Victoria Cross was established in 1856 to recognise acts of valour during the Crimean War.

17. A. Around 5% of UK population lives in Wales.

18. A. By 1400, in England, official documents were being written in English and English had become the preferred language of the royal court and Parliament.

19. B, D. Dame Barbara Mary Quant is a British fashion designer and fashion icon. She became an instrumental figure in the 1960s London-based Mod and youth fashion movements. Alexander McQueen was an English fashion designer and couturier. He was chief designer at Givenchy from 1996 to 2001.

20. A. the House of Lancaster had a red rose.

21. A. George Stephenson and his son Robert developed railway engines. Their Locomotion No. 1 was the first steam locomotive to carry passengers on a public rail line, the Stockton and Darlington Railway in 1825.

22. C. In the late 6th century, a man named Augustine was sent from Rome to England to bring Christianity to the Anglo-Saxons

23. C. Motor-car racing started in the UK in 1902.

24. B. Many English and Scottish protestants came to settle in Ulster during the 16th and 17th centuries.

TEST 13

1. Who died at the Battle of Trafalgar?

A.   Nelson

B.   Napoleon

C.   Oliver Cromwell

D.   Henry VIII

2. What was the first war to be extensively covered by the media?

A.   The Boer War

B.   The First World War

C.   The Second World War

D.   The Crimean War

3. In 1745, who was supported by Scottish Highlands clansmen and raised an army?

A.   Bonnie Prince Charlie

B.   Robert Burns

C.   Oliver Cromwell

D.   Kenneth MacAlpin

4. How many times has the UK hosted the Olympic games?

A.   1

B.   3

C.   4

D.   0

5. Which of the following line comes from the National Anthem?

A.   We shall never surrender

B.   God save our gracious Queen!

C.   She has a Lion heart

D.   The darling buds of May

6. Who made the first coins to be minted in Britain?

A.   The people of the Stone Age

B.   The Anglo-Saxons

C.   The people of the Iron Age

D.   The Romans

7. Who was born in Stratford-upon-Avon?

A.   Jane Austen

B.   Charles Dickens

C.   William Shakespeare

D.   Thomas Hardy

8. What was the last battle between Great Britain and France?

A.   The Battle of Trafalgar

B.   The Battle of Waterloo

C.   The Battle of Hastings

D.   Battle of Agincourt

9. Which invention was crucial to Britain's growth during the Industrial Revolution?

A.   Magnetic Resonance Imaging

B.   Steam power

C.   Radar

D.   Hovercraft

10. What stories are associated with Geoffrey Chaucer?

A.   The Cambridge Tales

B.   The Eastbourne Tales

C.   The Canterbury Tales

D.   The London Tales

11. During the reign of Charles II parts of London were destroyed, what was the cause of this destruction?

A.   A war

B.   A flood

C.   A fire

D.   An earthquake

12. What is meant by The Enlightenment?

A.   A period of total peace in England

B.   A period when new ideas about politics, philosophy and science were developed

C.   A period when England became the largest empire the world had ever seen

D.   A period of economic recovery after the Second World War

13. The Falkland Islands are part of Great Britain.

A.   True

B.   False

14. Who is the patron Saint of Scotland?

A.   St David   C.   St George
B.   St Patrick   D.   St Andrew

15. Who appoints life peers in the House of Lords?

A.   The Speaker   C.   The Prime Minister
B.   The Archbishop of Canterbury   D.   The Monarch

16. Where is the Tate Art Gallery located?

A.   Glasgow   C.   London
B.   Cardiff   D.   Belfast

17. Boudicca, was a tribal leader from which tribe?

A.   The Romans   C.   The Anglo-Saxons
B.   The Vikings   D.   The Iceni

18. What is the name of the UK currency?

A.   Euro   C.   Peso
B.   Pound Sterling   D.   Dollar

19. Who became British Prime Minister in 1945?

A.   Clement Attlee   C.   Harold Wilson
B.   Winston Churchill   D.   Harold Macmillan

20. Where is Snowdonia located?

A.   Scotland   C.   England
B.   Wales   D.   Northern Ireland

21. Who was the first female Prime Minister of the UK?

A.   Mary Stuart

B.   Theresa May

C.   Margaret Thatcher

D.   Florence Nightingale

22. Nick Park has won four Oscars for his animated films, including three for:

A.   Chariots of Fire

B.   Wallace and Gromit

C.   Four Weddings and a Funeral

D.   Women in Love

23. When was England ruled by a republic and not by a monarch?

A.   When Elizabeth I died without any successor

B.   When Charles I was executed

C.   When the Carta Magna restricted the king's power

D.   When kind Harold died after the Battle of Hastings

24. Towns, cities and rural areas in the UK are governed by officials appointed by the government.

A.   True

B.   False

ANSWERS TO TEST 13

1. A. Admiral Nelson died during the battle of Trafalgar after being hit by a musket ball.

2. D. The Crimean War was the first war to be extensively covered by the media through news stories and photographs.

3. A. In 1745 there was another attempt to put a Stuart king back on the throne in place of George I's son, George II. Charles Edward Stuart (also called Bonnie Prince Charlie), the grandson of James II, landed in Scotland. He was supported by clansmen from the Scottish highlands and raised and army.

4. B. the Olympic games came to the UK 3 times. In 1908, 1948 and 2012.

5. B. The first verse of the National Anthem starts with the line: 'God save our gracious Queen! Long live our noble Queen!'

6. C. The oldest coins found date back to the Iron Age, between around 1200 and 600 BC.

7. C. William Shakespeare was an English playwright, born in Stratford-upon-Avon in 1564.

8. B. The Battle of Waterloo which, in 1815, saw the defeat of the Emperor Napoleon by the Duke of Wellington also marked the end of wars with France.

9. B. During the Industrial Revolution in the 18th and 19th centuries, Britain was the first country to industrialise on a large scale. This revolution was supported by the development of steam power to run heavy machinery.

10. C. Geoffrey Chaucer wrote a series of poems in the 14th century about a group of people going to Canterbury on a pilgrimage. They are called The Canterbury Tales.

11. C. The Great Fire of London swept through the central parts of London for 4 days in September 1666.

12. B. The Age of Enlightenment was an intellectual, scientific and philosophical movement in the 17th and 18th centuries that developed many new ideas across Europe.

13. B. False. The Falklands islands are overseas territories.

14. D. St Andrew is the patron Saint of Scotland.

15. D. Life peers are appointed by the Monarch on the advice of the Prime Minister.

16. C. The Tate Britain and Tate Modern are museums located in London.

17. D. Boudica was a queen of the British Iceni tribe who led an uprising against the conquering forces of the Roman Empire in AD 60.

18. B. The currency in the UK is the Pound Sterling.

19. A. in 1945, a Labour government was elected, and Clement Atlee became Prime Minister.

20. B. Snowdonia is a region in northwest Wales concentrated around the mountains and glacial landforms of massive Snowdonia National Park.

21. C. Margaret Thatcher was Prime Minister of the United Kingdom from 1979 to 1990, she was the first woman to hold that office.

22. B. Nick Park is a British animator, director, producer and writer who created Wallace and Gromit.

23. B. When Charles I was executed, England declared itself a republic, called the Commonwealth. It no longer had a Monarch.

24. B. False. Towns, cities and rural areas in the UK are governed by democratically elected councils, often called local authorities.

TEST 14

1. Who is the patron Saint of Northern Ireland?

A.   St George

B.   St Patrick

C.   St Andrew

D.   St David

2. In 1776, which British colonies declared their independence?

A.   North African

B.   Asian

C.   North American

D.   South African

3. Which territory is not a part of Great Britain?

A.   Wales

B.   Northern Ireland

C.   England

D.   Scotland

4. How often are general elections held in the UK?

A.   Every 3 years

B.   Every 4 years

C.   Every 5 years

D.   Every 10 years

5. What sort of church is the Church of Scotland?

A.   Catholic

B.   Baptist

C.   Presbyterian

D.   Methodist

6. What is the Queen's speech about during the opening of the UK Parliament?

A.   What the Royal family did the previous year.

B.   What the Government did the previous year.

C.   What business matters the Royal family will conduct in the year ahead.

D.   What the Government policies will be in the year ahead.

7. It is compulsory for 16 and 17-year-olds to join the National Citizen Service.

A.   True   B.   False

8. What is the Cenotaph?

A.   A flower   C.   A war memorial
B.   A Christian church   D.   A theatre

9. When is St George's day?

A.   17th March   C.   1st March
B.   30th November   D.   23rd April

10. Who was the father of Queen Elizabeth I?

A.   Edward I   C.   Henry VII
B.   Henry V   D.   Henry VIII

11. There are 15 national parks in England, Wales and Scotland. What are they?

A.   Giant greenhouses   C.   Areas of protected countryside
B.   Land formations of columns made   D.   Medieval buildings
from volcanic lava

12. Which flower is associated with Wales?

A.   Daffodil   C.   Shamrock
B.   Rose   D.   Thistle

13. The assassination of the Archduke Franz Ferdinand of Austria in 1914 led to which of the following wars?

A.   The Crimean War   C.   The Civil War
B.   The First World War   D.   The Second World War

14. The Bill of Rights of 1689 ensure the right to a fair trial.

A.   True   B.   False

15. Who is the heir to the throne of Britain?

A.   The Prince of Wales   C.   The Prince of Edinburgh

B.   The Prince of Cambridge   D.   The Duke of York

16. What happened to Mary, Queen of Scots, after being sent to prison for 20 years by her cousin Queen Elizabeth I?

A.   She got married.   C.   She was executed.

B.   She was sent to France.   D.   She was sent to Scotland.

17. Northern Ireland and Scotland have their own banknotes.

A.   True   B.   False

18. What is the period called the swinging sixties known for?

A.   A downgrade in manufacturing   C.   A shortage of water

B.   A growth in British fashion and pop   D.   A blockage of social laws
music

19. How often are 'Prime Minister's Questions' held in the parliament?

A.   Every day   C.   Every two weeks

B.   Every week   D.   Once a month

20. Which of the following statements is TRUE:

A.   Mary Stuart was Protestant   B.   Mary Stuart was Catholic

21. Who was William Caxton?

A. A poet who wrote about a group of people going to Canterbury on a pilgrimage

B. The first person in England to print books using a printing press

C. The first person to sail singlehanded around the world

D. The inventor of the television

22. Wales has its own established church.

A. True

B. False

23. Who chairs the debates at the House of Commons?

A. A Bishop

B. The Prime Minister

C. The Speaker

D. A Lord

24. Who became Prime Minister after Margaret Thatcher?

A. James Callaghan

B. John Major

C. Tony Blair

D. Harold Wilson

ANSWERS TO TEST 14

1. B. Saint Patrick is the primary patron saint of Ireland and Northern Ireland.

2. C. In 1776, 13 North American colonies declared their independence, stating that people had a right to establish their own governments.

3. B. Northern Ireland is in the UK but not in Great Britain.

4. C. The Fixed-term Parliaments Act 2011 sets the next date of the general election at a five-year interval on the first Thursday of May.

5. C. The National Church of Scotland is a Presbyterian Church

6. D. One of the Queen's ceremonial roles is to open the annual parliamentary session with a speech which summarises the government's policies for the year ahead.

7. B. False. The National Citizen Service programme is voluntary.

8. C. The Cenotaph is a war memorial located in London. It was erected after the end of World War 1.

9. D. St George's day, patron of England, is celebrated on the 23rd of April.

10. D. Queen Elizabeth I was the daughter of Henry VIII and Anne Boleyn.

11. C. National Parks are areas of protected countryside that everyone can visit, and where people live, work and look after the landscape.

12. A. The daffodil is one of Wales national symbols, with the red dragon and the leek.

13. B. The assassination of the Archduke Franz Ferdinand of Austria in June 1914 set World War 1 in motion.

14. B. False. The Bill of Rights, confirmed the rights of Parliament and the limits of the king's power.

15. A. Prince of Wales is a title traditionally and ceremonially granted to the heir apparent of the British throne.

16. C. Mary, Queen of Scots, was executed in 1587 for plotting against Elizabeth I.

17. A. True. Both Northern Ireland and Scotland have their own banknotes. They are in Pound and valid throughout the UK.

18. B. The Swinging Sixties was a youth-driven cultural revolution that took place in the UK during the mid-to-late 1960s. It saw a flourishing in art, music and fashion.

19. B. Prime Minister's Question Time, also referred to as PMQs, gives MPs the chance to question the Prime Minister. It takes place at midday every Wednesday when the Commons is sitting.

20. B. Mary Stuart, Queen of Scots was catholic.

21. B. William Caxton was an English merchant, diplomat, and writer. He is thought to be the first person to introduce a printing press into England, in 1476.

22. B. False. The Church in Wales is the Anglican Church, as in England.

23. C. Debates in the House of Commons are chaired by the Speaker.

24. B. John Major succeeded Margaret Thatcher in 1990.

TEST 15

1. In 1314 the Scottish, led by Robert the Bruce, defeated the English at the battle of Bannockburn, and Scotland remained unconquered by the English.

A.   True   B.   False

2. In the UK, you have to be 21 years old to be able to vote in a general election.

A.   True   B.   False

3. Which flower is associated with Scotland?

A.   Shamrock.   C.   Daffodil

B.   Rose   D.   Thistle

4. Which of the following wars took place between 1899 and 1902 in South Africa?

A.   The Hundred Years War   C.   The First World War

B.   The Boer War   D.   The Crimean War

5. Who was the first man in the world to run 1 mile in under 4 minutes?

A.   Sir Chris Hoy   C.   David Weir

B.   Sir Roger Bannister   D.   Mo Farah

6. What is the name of the area in London where famous theatres are located?

A.   Soho   C.   Westminster

B.   Theatreland   D.   Hyde Park

7. Which king was executed in 1649?

A.   Henry VIII

B.   James I

C.   Elizabeth I

D.   Charles I

8. Isambard Kingdom Brunel is known for:

A.   The construction of the Great Western Railway

B.   The invention of the television

C.   The construction of the Tower of London

D.   The discovery of DNA

9. What is "the Proms"?

A.   An annual music awards ceremony

B.   An annual cultural festival which includes music, dance, and art

C.   A summer festival of daily classical music concerts

D.   Light-hearted comedy and theatre

10. What was invented by Alan Turing in the 1930s?

A.   The jet engine

B.   The television

C.   The Turing machine

D.   The ball pen

11. Who designed the Cenotaph?

A.   Sir Norman Foster

B.   Dame Zaha Hadid

C.   Sir Edwin Lutyens

D.   Isambard Kingdom Brunel

12. Who was the British scientist who co-discovered the structure of the DNA molecule in the 1950s?

A.   Sir Ian Wilmot

B.   Keith Campbell

C.   James Watt

D.   Francis Crick

13. When did the UK join the EU?

A.   In 1957

B.   In 1973

C.   In 2016

D.   In 1964

14. When is St Andrew's day celebrated?

A.   17th April

B.   31st December

C.   1st March

D.   30th November

15. MPs can be contacted at their office in the House of Commons.

A.   True

B.   False

16. Who became famous for his tramp character in silent movies?

A.   Sir Rex Harrison

B.   David Niven

C.   Richard Burton

D.   Charlie Chaplin

17. What sort of sport is the Grand National?

A.   Rugby

B.   Golf

C.   Horse Racing

D.   Tennis

18. Who was voted the greatest Briton of all time in 2002?

A.   Isaac Newton

B.   Winston Churchill

C.   Alexander Fleming

D.   Mo Farat

19. What did Emmeline Pankhurst fight for?

A.   The right to liberty and security

B.   The right for women to vote

C.   Freedom of expression

D.   The right to a fair trial

20. Which two political parties formed a coalition in 2010?

A.   The Conservative Party

B.   The Green Party

C.   The Labour Party

D.   The Liberal Democrat Party

21. Under which name was the movement of opinion against the authority of the Pope during the times of Henry VIII known?

A. The Spanish Inquisition

B. The Holy Wars

C. The Reformation

D. The Enlightenment

22. Where is the Lake District National Park located?

A. Scotland

B. Wales

C. England

D. Northern Ireland

23. In the 17th century, William of Orange was asked by Protestants to invade England and proclaim himself king. The invasion met no resistance. This event was known as:

A. The 'Glorious Revolution'

B. The Restoration

C. The 'Great Depression'

D. The 'Blitz'

24. Who was reigning in England when English settlers first began to colonise the eastern coast of America?

A. Queen Victoria

B. Henry VIII

C. Elizabeth I

D. Charles II

ANSWERS TO TEST 15

1. A. True. That is correct, Scottish leader Robert the Bruce, defeated the English at the battle of Bannockburn in 1314.

2. B. False. In the UK, the voting age is 18.

3. D. The official flower of Scotland is the thistle.

4. B. The Boer War was a conflict fought between the British Empire and the two Boer Republics over the Empire's influence in Southern Africa from 1899 to 1902.

5. B. In 1954, Sir Roger Bannister became the first man in the world to run a mile in under four minutes.

6. B. The West end of London where most theatres are located is also called Theatreland.

7. D. Charles I was accused of treason and beheaded in 1649.

8. A. Isambard Kingdom Brunel was an engineer from the 19th century. He developed the Great Western Railway, the first major railway built in Britain which runs from Paddington Station in London to the southwest of England, the West Midlands and Wales.

9. C. The Proms is a summer festival of classical music that takes place mostly in the Royal Albert Hall in London.

10. C. Turing developed the Turing machine in the 1930's, a theoretical model that helped create computers.

11. C. The Cenotaph was designed by sir Edwin Lutyens.

12. D. Francis Crick was a British molecular biologist, biophysicist, and neuroscientist. He

played a crucial role in deciphering the helical structure of the DNA molecule.

13. B. The UK joined the European Union in 1973.

14. D. St Andrew's day, patron of Scotland, is celebrated on the 30th of November.

15. A. True. Members of the public can contact their MP by writing to them in their office in the House of Commons, or to their office in the constituency.

16. D. Charles Spencer Chaplin was an English comic actor, filmmaker, and composer who rose to fame in the era of silent film. He became a worldwide icon through his screen persona, the Tramp.

17. C. The Grand National is a horse race held annually at Aintree Racecourse in Liverpool, England

18. B. In a nationwide BBC poll, attracting more than a million voters, Winston Churchill was voted the greatest Briton of all time.

19. B. In 1903, Emmeline Pankhurst helped create the Women's Social and Political Union also called suffragettes. The group fought for women's right to vote, which they finally obtained in 1918.

20. A, D. In May 2010, the Conservative and Liberal Democrat parties formed a coalition government.

21. C. The English Reformation took place in 16th-century England after Henry VIII broke away from the authority of the Pope.

22. C. The Lake District is a National Park in Cumbria, in northwest England.

23. A. The Glorious Revolution refers to the events of 1688–89 that saw King James II of England deposed and succeeded by one of his daughters, Mary, and her husband William.

24. C. The first English settlers arrived in America during the reign of Elizabeth I.

TEST 16

1. William Wordsworth wrote a poem about which national flower?

A.   Rose

B.   Daffodil

C.   Thistle

D.   Shamrock

2. During the Middle Ages, who were the serfs?

A.   Peasants who worked an area of land

B.   Soldiers who fought for the king

C.   Noblemen part of king's council

D.   A group of skilled people who built cathedrals

3. How old do citizens of the UK have to be to stand for public office?

A.   18

B.   21

C.   16

D.   25

4. Which of the following is a key roles of school governors?

A.   Monitoring student's behaviour

B.   Setting the strategic direction of the school

C.   Recruit teachers

D.   Giving awards to the best students of the school

5. When did the Emancipation Act abolished slavery throughout the British Empire?

A.   16th century

B.   17th century

C.   18th century

D.   19th century

6. Who established the Church of England?

A. Henry VIII

B. Oliver Cromwell

C. Winston Churchill

D. William of Orange

7. What led the American colonies to want their independence from Britain?

A. The British government wanted to control their borders

B. They were running out of resources

C. The British wanted to tax them

D. There were not enough jobs for the local people

8. When did the First World War end?

A. 12.00 pm on 11th November 1914

B. 12.00 pm on 11th November 1918

C. 11.00 am on 11th November 1914

D. 11.00 am on 11th November 1918

9. Who is the head of the Church of England?

A. The Prime Minister

B. The Archbishop of Canterbury

C. The Pope

D. The Monarch

10. What is the most famous tennis tournament played in the UK?

A. The Queen's Club Championships

B. Wimbledon

C. Roland Garros

D. The Aegon Championships

11. What did 'the Butler Act' introduce in 1944?

A. Free primary education in England, Wales and Scotland

B. Free university fees in England, Wales, Scotland and Northern Ireland

C. Free primary and secondary education in England, Wales and Scotland

D. Free secondary education in England and Wales

12. What is the minimum age required to serve on a jury?

A. 16

B. 18

C. 21

D. 25

13. The Man Booker Prize is awarded in which of the following categories?

A.   Films   C.   Literature

B.   Sport   D.   Music

14. What is the name of Irish people who favoured complete independence from the UK in the 19th century?

A.   Fenians   C.   Highlanders

B.   Quakers   D.   Suffragettes

15. When is Boxing Day?

A.   1st day of the year   C.   26th of December

B.   1st of April   D.   21st of June

16. Who led a team of scientists to 'split the atom' for the first time?

A.   Alexander Fleming   C.   Ernest Rutherford

B.   Alan Turing   D.   Sir Peter Mansfield

17. Which novel by JRR Tolkien was voted the country's best-loved novel in 2003?

A.   Oliver Twist   C.   Pride and Prejudice

B.   James Bond   D.   The Lord of the Rings

18. What is the name of the process by which many Scottish landlords destroyed individual small farms to make space for large flocks of sheep and cattle?

A.   The Black Death   C.   The Highland Clearances

B.   The Corn Removal   D.   The Enlightenment

19. When was the Domesday Book written?

A.   After the Viking invasion   C.   After the last Roman invasion

B.   After the Norman conquest   D.   After the Anglo-Saxon invasion

20. By law, which of these media must give a balanced coverage of all political parties and viewpoints before an election?

A. Television

B. Internet

C. Newspapers

D. Billboards

21. Who developed the radar?

A. John Logie Baird

B. Sir Frank Whittle

C. Sir Christopher Cockrell

D. Sir Robert Watson-Watt

22. What battle is commemorated in the Bayeux Tapestry?

A. The Battle of Waterloo

B. The Battle of Trafalgar

C. The Battle of Hastings

D. The Battle of Britain

23. What sort of election occurs when a member of the Parliament dies or resigns?

A. Coalition

B. Pre-selection

C. Random selection

D. By-election

24. What charity works to preserve important buildings, coastline and countryside in England?

A. Shelter

B. Age UK

C. Crisis

D. The National Trust

220

ANSWERS TO TEST 16

1. B. "I Wandered Lonely as a Cloud" is a lyric poem by William Wordsworth. It was inspired by daffodils.

2. A. Serfs were peasants who worked an area of their lord's land.

3. A. In the UK, citizens aged 18 or over can stand for public office.

4. B. Governors have three key roles: setting the strategic direction of the school, ensuring accountability, and monitoring and evaluating school performance.

5. D. The Emancipation Act also called the Slavery Abolition Act was signed in 1833 and started the immediate abolition of slavery in most parts of the British Empire.

6. A. Henry VIII established the Church of England in 1534 after breaking from the authority of the Pope.

7. C. By 1773, Britain had imposed heavy taxes on its American colonies. The British Tea Act of 1773, although not a direct tax, angered the colonists and ignited the insurrection that lead to American colonies' independence in 1776.

8. D. It was decided to be on the 11th hour of the 11th day of the 11th month. 11 November 1918 at 11 AM.

9. D. The Monarch is the head of the Church of England.

10. B. Wimbledon is the oldest tennis tournament in the world.

11. D. Richard Butler became Education Secretary in 1941. He introduced free secondary education in England and Wales in 1944.

12. B. One must be at least 18 to serve on a jury.

13. C. The Booker Prize is a literary prize awarded each year for the best novel written in English and published in the United Kingdom or Ireland.

14. A. The Fenian Brotherhood, secret political organisations in the late 19th and early 20th century was dedicated to the establishment of an independent Irish Republic.

15. C. Boxing Day comes the day after Christmas, December 26th.

16. C. Between 1914 and 1919, Ernest Rutherford conducted many experiments by bombarding nitrogen gas with alpha particles that lead to the description of "splitting the atom".

17. D. During The Big Read, a 2003 survey on books carried out by the BBC. The UK voted Tolkien's The Lord of the Rings best-loved novel.

18. C. The Highland Clearances were the evictions of a significant number of tenants in the Scottish Highlands and Islands, mostly from 1750 to 1860.

19. B. After the 1066 Norman conquest, William the Conqueror ordered a survey of England and parts of Wales, recorded in the Domesday Book.

20. A. By law, radio and television coverage of the political parties must be balanced and so equal time has to be given to rival viewpoints.

21. D. Sir Robert Watson-Watt developed radar technology in the 1930's

22. C. The Bayeux Tapestry is an embroidered cloth nearly 70 metres long that depicts the events leading up to the Norman conquest of England and culminating in the Battle of Hastings.

23. D. If an MP dies or resigns, there will be a fresh election, called a by-election, in their constituency.

24. D. The National Trust is a charity for heritage, conservation, and preservation in England, Wales and Northern Ireland.

TEST 17

1. Which armed force fought the Battle of Britain during WWII?

A.   The Royal Navy

B.   The Police Force

C.   The Naval Service

D.   The Royal Air Force

2. Haggis is a traditional food from which area?

A.   Wales

B.   England

C.   Northern Ireland

D.   Scotland

3. Who were the first people to live in Britain in what we call the Stone Age?

A.   Farmers

B.   Peasants

C.   Hunter-gatherers

D.   Pirates

4. Anyone who is violent towards their partner – whether they are a man or a woman, married or living together – can be prosecuted.

A.   True

B.   False

5. What is the capital city of Scotland?

A.   Glasgow

B.   St Andrews

C.   Edinburgh

D.   Aberdeen

6. Why was the British promised 'Home Rule' for Ireland, delayed until 1921?

A.   Due to the outbreak of the First World War

B.   Due to the outbreak of the Second World War

C.   Because there was not a king on the British throne

D.   Due to the outbreak of the Black Death

7. Which of the following poets was inspired by nature?

A.   John Masefield   C.   Siegfried Sassoon

B.   Wilfred Owen   D.   William Wordsworth

8. How often are the members of the Welsh Parliament elected?

A.   Every 2 years   C.   Every 4 years

B.   Every 3 years   D.   Every 5 years

9. James I was King of which country before becoming King of England?

A.   Wales   C.   France

B.   Ireland   D.   Scotland

10. Which of the following charities helps protect children?

A.   NSPCC   C.   Friends of the Earth

B.   Shelter   D.   Crisis

11. What is the Turner Prize?

A.   A literature award   C.   A contemporary art award

B.   A music award   D.   A theatre award

12. Where was Anne Boleyn, the wife of Henry VIII, executed?

A.   Houses of the Parliament   C.   Tower of London

B.   Stonehenge   D.   Whitehall

13. When was the Magna Carta agreed by the king?

A.   1652   C.   1215

B.   1585   D.   1066

14. Which film produced in the UK was one of the most commercially successful films of all time and one of the highest-grossing film franchises?

A.   Harry Potter   C.   The Lord of the Rings

B.   Spider-man   D.   Indiana Jones

15. What is the capital city of Northern Ireland?

A.   Cork   C.   Belfast

B.   Edinburgh   D.   Dublin

16. Which of the following statements is true:

A.   Elizabeth I was a Protestant and she   B.   Elizabeth I was a Catholic and she
succeeded in finding a balance between   succeeded in finding a balance between
the views of the Catholics and the more   the views of the Catholics and the more
extreme Protestants.   extreme Protestants.

17. Between 1680 and 1720 many refugees called Huguenots came to England, which country did they come from?

A.   Pakistan   C.   India

B.   Germany   D.   France

18. What song is sung by people in the UK and other countries when they are celebrating the New Year?

A.   Auld Lang Syne   C.   Jingle Bells

B.   The British Anthem   D.   White Christmas

19. What was the religion of the Puritans?

A.   Hindu   C.   Sikh

B.   Catholic   D.   Protestant

20. Proceedings in Parliament are broadcast on television and published in official reports known as:

A.   Canvassing

B.   Hansard

C.   Cabinets

D.   Domesday Book

21. You have to be at least 21 years old to stand as MP.

A.   True

B.   False

22. When was the last successful foreign invasion of England?

A.   1415

B.   1314

C.   1066

D.   1200

23. What is the Commonwealth?

A.   An organization responsible for the protection and promotion of human rights in its member countries.

B.   A group of European and North American countries that have agreed to help each other if they come under attack.

C.   An association of countries that support each other and work together towards shared goals in democracy and development.

D.   An international organization that aims to prevent war and promote international peace and security.

24. Who supported King Charles I during the Civil War?

A.   Roundheads

B.   Suffragettes

C.   Quakers

D.   Cavaliers

ANSWERS TO TEST 17

1. D. The Royal Air Force fought and won against the German planes of the Luftwaffe in 1940.

2. D. Haggis is a Scottish savoury pudding containing sheep's pluck, onions and spice.

3. C. The first people to live in Britain were hunter-gatherers.

4. A. True. Anyone who is violent towards their partner – whether they are a man or a woman, married or living together – can be prosecuted.

5. C. Edinburgh is the capital city of Scotland.

6. A. The outbreak of the First World War led the British government to postpone any changes in Ireland.

7. D. William Wordsworth was an English Romantic poet of the 18th century referred to as the "Poet of nature".

8.C. The members of the Welsh Parliament are elected for 4 years.

9. D. When Elizabeth I died, her cousin James VI of Scotland became also King James I of England, Wales and Ireland.

10. A. The National Society for the Prevention of Cruelty to Childrenv(NSPCC) is a British child protection charity.

11. C. The Turner Prize is an annual prize presented to a contemporary British visual artist.

12. C. In 1536, Anne Boleyn was accused of taking lovers. She was executed at the Tower of London.

13. C. Magna Carta, is a royal charter of rights agreed to by King John of England at Runnymede, near Windsor, on 15 June 1215.

14. A. Harry Potter is a film series based on the eponymous novels by J. K. Rowling and one of the most successful franchises produced in the UK.

15. C. Belfast is the capital city of Northern Ireland.

16. A. Elizabeth I was a Protestant and she succeeded in finding a balance between the views of the Catholics and the more extreme Protestants.

17. D. Huguenots were French Protestants in the 16th and 17th centuries, many of which fled to England.

18. A. The song Auld Lang Syne is sung by people in the UK to celebrate the New Year.

19. D. The Puritans were a group of Protestants who advocated strict and simple religious doctrine and worship.

20. B. Hansard (also called the Official Report) is the edited verbatim report of proceedings of both the House of Commons and the House of Lords. It is published daily.

21. B. False. Anyone aged 18 or over can stand for election as an MP.

22. C. The Norman Conquest in 1066 was the last successful foreign invasion of England.

23. C. The Commonwealth is an association of countries that support each other and work together towards shared goals in democracy and development. Most member states were once part of the British Empire, although a few countries which were not have also joined.

24. D. During the civil war between the king and Parliament the Cavaliers supported the king while the Roundheads supported the Parliament.

TEST 18

1. How old do you have to be to buy alcohol in the UK?

A. 17

B. 18

C. 19

D. 20

2. Where does the UK Parliament sit?

A. Westminster

B. Stormont

C. Holyrood

D. Senedd

3. Which of the following tribes invaded Britain?

A. The Jutes

B. The Angles

C. The Saxons

D. All of the above

4. Which of the following is NOT the responsibility of the MPs?

A. Scrutinise the government

B. Represent their constituency

C. Protect life and property

D. Debate important national issues

5. Which hill fort from the Iron Age can be seen in the county of Dorset?

A. Conwy Castle

B. Caernarfon Castle

C. Edinburgh Castle

D. Maiden Castle

6. What was the name of Sir Francis Drake's ship and which was one of the first to sail around the world?

A. The Golden Eye

B. The Golden Hind

C. Elizabeth

D. The Sharp

7. The system of land ownership used by the Normans was called:

A.   Clergy

B.   Chartism

C.   Feudalism

D.   Imperialism

8. Which island is located between England and Northern Ireland but is not in the UK?

A.   The Isle of Man

B.   Malta

C.   Jersey

D.   Fiji

9. What sort of stories were collected in the Canterbury Tales by Geoffrey Chaucer?

A.   Love stories

B.   Children's stories

C.   Travellers' stories

D.   War stories

10. Hanukkah is a Jewish festival to remember the Jews' struggle for religious freedom.

A.   True

B.   False

11. The Prime Minister has a country house outside London called:

A.   Sparkle

B.   Downing

C.   Windsor

D.   Chequers

12. Who is the author of the famous play 'Macbeth'?

A.   Alexander Thomas

B.   William Shakespeare

C.   Harold Pinter

D.   Evelyn Waugh

13. How many pence are there in a pound?

A.   100 pence

B.   50 pence

C.   60 pence

D.   10 pence

14. When did the UK sign the European Convention of Human Rights?

A.   1940

B.   1945

C.   1950

D.   1973

15. What does the NATO stand for?

A. The North American Transparent Organisation

C. The North Atlantic Treaty Organisation

B. The North Atlantic Trust Organisation

D. The North American Treaty Organisation

16. If you are self-employed:

A. You need to pay your own tax

C. You don't need to pay tax

B. Tax is automatically taken from your earnings by a specialised agency

D. You only needed to pay tax on 50% of your earnings

17. Which British painter is considered to be the artist who raised the profile of landscape painting?

A. Joseph Turner

C. John Constable

B. David Allan

D. Sir John Lavery

18. In which city is the Millennium Stadium located?

A. Birmingham

C. Liverpool

B. Nottingham

D. Cardiff

19. What was the population of the UK in 1700?

A. 1 million

C. 5 million

B. 14 million

D. 20 million

20. Who gave Henry VIII the son he wanted, Edward?

A. Jane Seymour

C. Anne of Cleves

B. Catherine of Aragon

D. Catherine Parr

21. Which of the following countries is NOT a member of the Commonwealth?

A. Ghana

C. Greece

B. Cyprus

D. Sierra Leone

22. How many American colonies declared their independence in 1776, stating that people had a right to establish their own governments?

A. 11   C. 13

B. 12   D. 14

23. Which of the following contains great examples of stained glass?

A. York Minster   C. Hadrian's Wall

B. Bayeux Tapestry   D. Magna Carta

24. In which city is Holyrood located?

A. Edinburgh   C. Aberdeen

B. Belfast   D. Glasgow

ANSWERS TO TEST 18

1. B. It is a criminal offence to sell alcohol to anyone who is under 18 or to buy alcohol for people who are under the age of 18.

2. A. The UK parliament sits in Westminster.

3. D. The Roman army left Britain in AD 410. Britain was again invaded by tribes from northern Europe: the Jutes, the Angles and the Saxons.

4. C. MPs don't protect lives but they have a number of different responsibilities. They represent everyone in their constituency, help to create new laws, scrutinize and comment on what the government is doing and debate important national issues.

5. D. Maiden Castle is an Iron Age hill in the English county of Dorset.

6. B. Golden Hind was a galleon captained by Francis Drake in his circumnavigation of the world between 1577 and 1580.

7. C. In the Middle Ages, the Norman used feudalism, a social system in which people worked and fought for nobles who gave them protection and the use of land in return.

8. A. The Isle of Man is close to the UK but is not a part of it.

9. C. In the years leading up to 1400, Geoffrey Chaucer wrote The Canterbury Tales, a series of stories from about a group of people travelling to Canterbury on a pilgrimage.

10. A. True. Hanukkah is a Jewish festival hat reaffirms the ideals of Judaism and commemorate the recovery of Jerusalem in the 2nd century BCE.

11. D. Chequers, or Chequers Court, is the country house of the Prime Minister of the United Kingdom.

12. B. Macbeth is a tragedy by William Shakespeare thought to have been first performed in 1606.

13. A. A pound counts 100 pence.

14. C. The UK was one of the first countries to sign the European Convention of Human Rights in 1950.

15. C. NATO stands for The North Atlantic Treaty Organisation.

16. A. If you are self-employed, you need to complete a self-assessment and pay your own tax.

17. A. Joseph Turner, born in 1775, was an influential landscape painter.

18. D. The Millennium Stadium is located in Cardiff.

19. C. The population of the UK in 1700 was around 5 million people.

20. A. in 1537, Jane Seymour finally gave Henry VIII the son he wanted, Edward.

21. D. Greece is not a member of the Commonwealth.

22. C. In 1776, 13 American colonies declared their independence, stating that people had a right to establish their own governments.

23. A. York Minster is a famous example of stained glass used on the windows of some cathedrals during the Middle Ages.

24. A. Holyrood is an area in Edinburgh, lying east of the city centre, and is known for hosting the Scottish Parliament building.

TEST 19

1. When is the anniversary of the Battle of the Boyne celebrated in Northern Ireland?

A.   March

B.   May

C.   June

D.   July

2. Which famous murder-mystery play has been running in the west end since 1952 and has had the longest initial run of any show in history?

A.   The Phantom of the Opera

B.   The Mousetrap

C.   Evita

D.   Jesus Christ Superstar

3. What was the ability of the Harrier jump jet aircraft?

A.   To carry 1,000 passengers

B.   To take off vertically

C.   To float on water

D.   To reach supersonic speeds

4. When did the development of a free press take place?

A.   1795

B.   1685

C.   1695

D.   1785

5. Which of the following is traditional British food?

A.   Pasta carbonara

B.   Green curry

C.   Tacos

D.   Fish and Chips

6. In the UK, if the jury finds a defendant guilty, the judge decides the penalty:

A.   True

B.   False

7. Who was the first person to print books using a printing press in England?

A. William Caxton C. John Barbour
B. Geoffrey Chaucer D. Jane Austen

8. The Scottish parliament cannot legislate on which of the following matters?

A. Health C. Immigration
B. Education D. Tax

9. Which of the following is the official church of the state?

A. The Church of Great Britain C. The Church of the United Kingdom
B. The Church of England D. The British Church

10. What is the official name of the country called the UK?

A. The United Kingdom of Great Britain and Southern Ireland. C. The United Kingdom of Great Britain and Northern Ireland.
B. The United Kingdom of Great Britain and Ireland. D. The United Kingdom and Great Ireland.

11. Which of the following is an ancient festival and has roots in the pagan festival to mark the beginning of winter?

A. Lent C. Halloween
B. Easter D. Hogmanay

12. How old was Edward VI, son of Henry VIII, when he died?

A. 15 years old C. 6 years old
B. 1 year old D. 37 years old

13. Where was Isaac Newton from?

A. Lincolnshire C. Cardiff
B. Stratford-upon-Avon D. Edinburgh

14. Who was the first person to lead a Roman invasion in Britain in 55 BC?

A.   Emperor Claudius

B.   Napoleon

C.   Julius Caesar

D.   William Caxton

15. What was the nickname given to the Scottish poet Robert Burns?

A.   The Great

B.   The Bard

C.   The Lover

D.   The Scottish

16. How long did the Hundred Years War between England and France really last for?

A.   100 years

B.   189 years

C.   74 years

D.   116 years

17. Who wrote the novel Charlie and the Chocolate Factory?

A.   Rudyard Kipling

B.   Sir William Golding

C.   Charles Dickens

D.   Roald Dahl

18. Which of the following is NOT a city of the UK?

A.   Belfast

B.   Newport

C.   Dublin

D.   Dundee

19. Which British explorer mapped the coast of Australia?

A.   Sake Dean Mahomet

B.   Richard Arkwright

C.   Captain James Cook

D.   Admiral Nelson

20. Which of the following is a traditional character of the pantomimes?

A.   The King

B.   The Dame

C.   A unicorn

D.   A mermaid

21. A National Insurance number proves to an employer that you have the right to work in the UK.

A.   True

B.   False

22. What names are associated to the landing in Normandy of Allied Forces during World War II? (select two)

A.   D-Day

B.   Domesday

C.   Operation Overlord

D.   Allies Day

23. What was the biggest source of employment in Britain before the 18th century?

A.   The ship industry

B.   Agriculture

C.   Teaching

D.   Manufacturing jobs

24. When was Ireland divided into two countries?

A.   In 1920

B.   In 1922

C.   In 1925

D.   In 1928

ANSWERS TO TEST 19

1. D. In Northern Ireland, the anniversary of the Battle of the Boyne is celebrated in July and is a public holiday.

2. B. The Mousetrap, a murder-mystery play by Dame Agatha Christie, has been running in the west end since 1952.

3. B. The Harrier jump jet is an aircraft capable of taking off vertically.

4. C. From 1695, newspapers were allowed to operate without a government licence. Increasing numbers of newspapers began to be published.

5. D. Fish and chips is a staple of traditional British food.

6. A. True. After a jury finds a defendant guilty, it is for the judge to decide which penalty should apply.

7. A. William Caxton was the first person to introduce a printing press in England in 1476.

8. C. The Scottish Parliament cannot legislate on matters of Immigration.

9. B. The official Church of the state is the Church of England or CoE.

10. C. The official name of the country is the United Kingdom of Great Britain and Northern Ireland.

11. C. Halloween, celebrated on 31st October, is rooted in a pagan festival to mark the beginning of winter.

12. A. Edward VI died at the age of 15 after ruling for just over six years. His half-sister Mary became queen.

13. A. Isaac Newton was born in 1643 in Lincolnshire, eastern England.

14. C. Julius Caesar led a Roman invasion of Britain in 55 BC but was unsuccessful.

15. B. Robert Burns, an 18th century Scottish poet, was known in Scotland as 'The Bard'.

16. D. From 1337, England fought a long war with France, called the Hundred Years War but that actually lasted 116 years.

17. D. Roald Dahl is the author of Charlie and the Chocolate Factory.

18. C. Dublin, capital of the Republic of Ireland, is not a city of the UK.

19. C. James Cook was a British explorer, navigator, cartographer, and captain in the British Royal Navy, famous for his three voyages between 1768 and 1779 in the Pacific Ocean and to Australia in particular.

20. B. One of the traditional characters of the pantomimes is the Dame, a woman played by a man.

21. B. False. The National Insurance number is used to keep track of your tax record and benefit entitlements. It doesn't prove your right to work.

22. A, C. On 6th of June 1944, the Allied invaded Normandy (France) during Operation Overlord. Often referred to as D-Day, it allowed the Allied forces to push through France and ultimately defeat the Nazis and put an end to WWII.

23. B. Before the 18th century, most people worked on farms and agriculture was the biggest source of employment in Britain.

24. B. The 1921 Anglo-Irish Treaty concluded the Irish war of independence and lead in 1922 to cut Ireland in two countries, the Irish Free State and Northern Ireland that remains a part of the UK.

TEST 20

1. Under which Act(s) was The Kingdom of Great Britain created?

A.   The Reform Act

B.   The Acts of Union

C.   The Emancipation Act

D.   The Butler Act

2. When did the post-war economic boom come to an end?

A.   In the early 1970s

B.   In the late 1970s

C.   In the early 1960s

D.   In the late 1960s

3. By 1200, the English ruled an area of Scotland known as the Pale, around Edinburgh:

A.   True

B.   False

4. What TWO names are given to the day before Lent?

A.   Pancake day

B.   Domesday

C.   Shrove Tuesday

D.   Ash Wednesday

5. The House of Commons is usually more independent of the government than the House of Lords:

A.   True

B.   False

6. Which prehistoric village has helped archaeologists to understand more about how people live near the end of the Stone Age?

A.   Stonehenge

B.   Scunthorpe

C.   Danelaw

D.   Skara Brae

7. Why was Mary known as "Bloody Mary"?

A.   She fought in numerous battles

B.   She persecuted Protestants

C.   She killed her father

D.   She put her sister in prison

8. When did Gordon Brown take over as Prime Minister from Tony Blair?

A.   In 2007

B.   In 2008

C.   In 2009

D.   In 2010

9. What marked the beginning of what is called 'constitutional monarchy'?

A.   The laws passed after the Glorious Revolution

B.   A speech given by the Queen

C.   The emergence of new ideas about politics, philosophy and science

D.   The development of the Bessemer process

10. The population is very equally distributed over the four parts of the UK:

A.   True

B.   False

11. What name is given to the elected members of the Northern Ireland Assembly?

A.   MSPs

B.   MLAs

C.   MPs

D.   AMs

12. Which of the following is a traditional Welsh food?

A.   Roast beef

B.   Welsh cakes

C.   Haggis

D.   Ulster fry

13. If you are found driving while exceeding the alcohol limit you will:

A.   Not be allowed to drive again

B.   Be taken to the hospital

C.   Be arrested

D.   Be taken home by the police

14. The UK is one of five permanent members of the UN Security Council:

A.   True   B.   False

15. What is the name of the first Danish king to rule in England?

A.   Canute   C.   Henry V

B.   Kenneth MacAlpin   D.   Edward I

16. To whom do new citizens swear or affirm loyalty during the citizenship ceremony?

A.   The Pope   C.   The Queen

B.   The Prime Minister   D.   The Church of England

17. Which of the following is a traditional pub game?

A.   Darts   C.   Bingo

B.   Hide and seek   D.   Checkers

18. Magistrates and Justices of the Peace (JPs) are members of:

A.   Government   C.   British Society

B.   Local community   D.   NHS

19. In 1837, Queen Victoria became queen of the UK at the age of 38.

A.   True   B.   False

20. Who makes the decisions on government policies in the UK?

A.   The Monarch   C.   The Prime Minister and the Cabinet

B.   Only the Prime Minister   D.   The Monarch and Prime Minister

21. In the early 20th century, what name was given to the activists who fought for women's right to vote?

A.   The Cavaliers   C.   The Roundheads

B.   The Suffragettes   D.   The Squareheads

22. Which of the following landmarks is the largest expanse of fresh water in mainland Britain?

A.   The River Thames

B.   Loch Lomond

C.   Loch Ness

D.   Lake District

23. Which Court deals with the serious criminal offences in England, Wales and Northern Ireland?

A.   The County Court

B.   The Crown Court

C.   The High Court

D.   The Sheriff Court

24. Where does the most famous sailing event in the UK take place?

A.   Holyhead, North Wales

B.   Cowes, The Isle of Wight

C.   Douglas, The Isle of Man

D.   Plymouth, England

ANSWERS TO TEST 20

1. B. The two Acts of Union signed in 1706 and 1707 created the United Kingdom of Great Britain.

2. B. The post-war economic boom seriously slowed down in the late 1970s.

3. B. False. By 1200, the English ruled an area of Ireland known as the Pale and situated around Dublin.

4. A, C. Shrove Tuesday is the day before Ash Wednesday, the start of Lent. In the UK, it is often celebrated by eating pancakes and is therefore also called Pancake Day.

5. B. False. It is the reverse. Because the House of Lords is not formed by general elections, it can be more independent of the government than the House of Commons.

6. D. Skara Brae is a stone-built Neolithic settlement, located on the Bay of Skaill on the west coast of Mainland, the largest island in the Orkney archipelago of Scotland.

7. B. Mary was a devout Catholic and persecuted Protestants.

8. A. Gordon Brown took over as Prime Minister from Tony Blair in 2007.

9. A. The laws passed after the Glorious Revolution mark the beginning of what is called 'constitutional monarchy'.

10. B. False. The population is very unequally distributed over the four parts of the UK. England makes up 84% of the total population, Wales around 5%, Scotland just over 8%, and Northern Ireland less than 3%.

11. B. Members of the Northern Ireland Assembly are known as MLAs or Members of the Legislative Assembly.

12. B. Welsh cakes are a traditional Welsh snack made from flour, dried fruits and spices, and served either hot or cold.

13. C. If you are found driving while exceeding the alcohol limit you will be arrested.

14. A. true. The UK is one of five permanent members of the United Nations Security Council.

15. A. Cnut, also known as Canute, was King of England, Denmark and Norway. As a Danish prince, Canute won the throne of England in 1016.

16. C. New citizens swear or affirm loyalty to the Queen as part of the citizenship ceremony.

17. A. Darts is a very traditional pub games.

18. B. Magistrates and Justices of the Peace (JPs) are members of the local community.

19. B. False. Victoria was 18 when she became Queen.

20. C. Decisions on government policies are made by the Prime Minister and the Cabinet.

21.B. A suffragette was a member of an activist women's organisation in the early 20th century who fought for and won the women's right to vote in public elections.

22. B. Loch Lomond is the largest expanse of fresh water in mainland Britain.

23. B. In England, Wales and Northern Ireland, serious criminal offences are tried in front of a judge and a jury in a Crown Court.

24. B. Cowes Week is one of the oldest and most respected regattas in the World. It takes place at Cowes on the Isle of Wight.

TEST 21

1. Which one of the following four changes did the Chartists NOT campaign for?

A. For any man to be able to stand as MP

B. Secret ballots

C. Annual elections for parliament

D. For MPs to be paid

2. Who was the first monarch of the House of Tudor?

A. King Richard III

B. Henry VII

C. Elizabeth I

D. James I

3. Which British playwright invented many common English words and had a great influence on the English language?

A. William Shakespeare

B. Graham Greene

C. Dylan Thomas

D. Harold Pinter

4. When was the first tennis club founded in the UK?

A. 1772

B. 1872

C. 1862

D. 1762

5. What British landmark was built as part of the UK's celebration of the new millennium?

A. The Tower of London

B. Tower Bridge

C. Westminster Abbey

D. The London Eye

6. What is the name of the action of handing out leaflets in the street or knocking on people's doors to ask for their political support?

A.	Shadowing	C.	Marketing
B.	Canvassing	D.	Persuasion

7. Which red flowers found on the battlefields of the First World War is usually worn during Remembrance Day?

A.	Roses	C.	Daffodils
B.	Poppies	D.	Carnations

8. What proportion of the population died as a result of the Black Death in England?

A.	Half of the population	C.	55% of the population
B.	One third of the population	D.	One quarter of the population

9. Where did slaves mainly come from during the slave trade?

A.	South America	C.	Southeast Asia
B.	West Africa	D.	North Africa

10. Who defeated the Vikings?

A.	King Alfred the Great	C.	Boudicca
B.	William I	D.	James II

11. Which of the following categories is recognised at the Laurence Olivier Awards?

A.	Music	C.	Sport
B.	Theatre	D.	Literature

12. What is the name of Admiral Nelson's flagship?

A.	HMS Victory	C.	Canute
B.	Golden Hind	D.	Grimsby

13. In Northern Ireland, a newly qualified driver must display an _____ plate for one year after passing the test.

A.   S

B.   N

C.   R

D.   L

14. How many crosses form the Union Flag?

A.   Two

B.   Three

C.   Four

D.   Five

15. Which of the following was a famous battles of the Hundred Years War?

A.   The Battle of Agincourt

B.   The Battle of Bannockburn

C.   The Battle of Culloden

D.   The Battle of Waterloo

16. What composer wrote music for King George I and for his son, George II?

A.   George Frederick Handel

B.   Gustav Holst

C.   Ralph Vaughan Williams

D.   Henry Purcell

17. When did Henry VIII become King?

A.   In April 1509

B.   In June 1497

C.   In March 1515

D.   In August 1495

18. What is the Old Bailey?

A.   A Famous criminal court

B.   A Scottish drink

C.   A traditional Welsh cake

D.   A British national park

19. Where can people facing domestic violence get help from?

A.   The NHS

B.   The Citizens Advise Bureau

C.   The Human Rights Commission

D.   The RSPB

20. Which of the following sports can be traced as far back as the Roman times?

A.   Tennis

B.   Football

C.   Horse racing

D.   Pool

21. Which American President worked closely with Margaret Thatcher?

A.   Hillary Clinton

B.   Ronald Reagan

C.   Jimmy Carter

D.   George Bush

22. What actions did Henry VII take after his victory in the Wars of the Roses?

A.   Reduced the power of the nobles

B.   Broke away with the Church of Rome

C.   Converted Britain to the Christianism

D.   Increased the power of the nobles

23. Which of the following meals can be prepared with bacon, eggs, sausage, black pudding, tomatoes, mushrooms, baked beans?

A.   Yorkshire pudding

B.   Haggis

C.   English breakfast

D.   Sunday roast

24. Which film was directed by David Lean?

A.   Breakfast at Tiffany's

B.   The 39 Steps

C.   Doctor Zhivago

D.   Chariots of Fire

ANSWERS TO TEST 21

1. C. The Chartists campaigned for annual elections for the parliament.

2. B. Henry VII (named Henry Tudor) was the first king of the House of Tudor.

3. A. William Shakespeare had a great influence on the English language and invented many words and expressions that are still commonly used today.

4. B. The first tennis club was founded in Leamington Spa in 1872.

5. D. The London Eye was originally built as part of the UK's celebration of the new millennium and continues to be an important part of New Year celebrations.

6. B. Canvassing is the systematic initiation of direct contact with individuals, commonly used during political campaigns for instance by handing out leaflets.

7. B. During Remembrance Day (11th of November) people wear a red poppy as a symbol of remembrance and hope for a peaceful future.

8. B. An estimated one third of the population of England died as a consequence of the Black Death pandemic of the 14th century.

9. B. Slaves came primarily from West Africa.

10. A. Alfred the Great was king of Wessex in the 9th century. He defeated the Viking army in 871.

11. B. The Laurence Olivier Awards recognise achievements in the area of theatre.

12. A. HMS Victory is a 104-gun ship launched in 1765. She is best known for her role as Lord Nelson's flagship at the Battle of Trafalgar in 1805.

13. C. In Northern Ireland, a newly qualified driver must display an 'R' plate (for restricted driver) for one year after passing the test.

14. B. The Union Flag has three crosses: St George's, St Andrew's and St Patrick's.

15. A. One of the most famous battles of the Hundred Years War was the Battle of Agincourt in 1415, where the English defeated the French.

16. A. George Frederick Handel was a German-British Baroque composer. In 1710, he became music director to the future King George I of Great Britain.

17. A. Henry VIII was king of England from April 1509 until his death on in 1547.

18. A. The Old Bailey is a criminal court building in central London, named after the street where it stands.

19. B. People facing domestic violence can get help from a solicitor or the Citizens Advice Bureau.

20. C. There is a very long history of horse racing in Britain, with evidence of events taking place as far back as Roman times.

21. B. Margaret Thatcher worked very closely with the United States President Ronald Reagan.

22. A. After his victory in the Wars of the Roses, Henry VII deliberately strengthened the central administration of England and reduced the power of the nobles to ensure that England remained peaceful and to secure his position as king.

23. C. The traditional full English breakfast is a substantial meal in the UK that centres around eggs, toasts, sausages, baked beans, and many other elements.

24. C. Doctor Zhivago is a 1965 epic historical and romantic drama film directed by David Lean.

This is it. You have worked hard and you are now ready to take the real test.

Now, it is time to celebrate all your hard work, have a drink, take a deep breath and pat yourself on the back. You will be walking to the testing centre with the confidence to pass.

Thank you for buying this guide and best of luck!

Please, feel free to leave a review and some feedback for this Book. Every little helps, I really appreciate that you decided to purchase this book. Your feedback will help improve future editions.

Thank you.

Hugh L.

Printed in Great Britain
by Amazon

21297069R00147